The Easter Rising of 1916 in North County Dublin

Withdrawn from Stock
Dublin City Public Libraries

D1614695

Maynooth Studies in Local History

SERIES EDITOR Raymond Gillespie

This volume is one of six Maynooth studies in local history published this year. Like the hundred or so that have preceded them, each has a task that is deceptively simple: to reconstruct and explain something of the realities of the local worlds that made up Ireland in the past. The apparent simplicity of this task conceals the considerable complexity and diversity of local societies that are revealed in these small books. Those local societies are not simply the expression of administrative units or geographical regions but social worlds that were carefully crafted and maintained in Ireland over time. That process of making local societies was one in which people interacted within their own spaces to create structures that made life workable on a day-to-day basis. They found common cause to hold together their local worlds but also sources of conflict that would sometimes drive them apart, as in 1916 when some communities were riven apart by violence and insurrection. The story of Skerries' involvement in 1916 provides a perspective on the contingent local processes in what is often seen as a purely national event. In the process of shaping local worlds people placed their own stamp on the things that they used to make daily life possible. Furniture and fittings in Borris House, for instance, reveal much about local perceptions of fashion and sociability and the role of women as architects in early nineteenth-century Ireland provides a distinctive insight into how spaces were ordered for living. Other sorts of local worlds were shaped in other ways. Estates had the potential to be the building blocks of local societies but often landlord priorities and those of the tenantry diverged, even when they had other features in common, as in the Gerrard estate in Galway. Elsewhere, large industrial operations, such as the Portmarnock Brick Works, might provide the basis of local societies. In the case of Dublin's South Circular Road people not only of diverse socio-economic backgrounds but also of different ethnic and religious origins were thrown together as a new suburb was created. At street corners and in churches they found ways to make local society work in a potentially divisive world threatened by the tensions leading up to the First World War.

Like previous titles in this series these small books recover the socially diverse worlds of urban and rural dwellers, men as well as women, and the rich occupants of great houses and evicted tenants. They often inhabited worlds that were little affected by the themes of national history, though that larger story often did impinge on their lives. Reconstructing those experiences is one of the challenges at the forefront of Irish historical research, and, in their own way, these studies convey the vibrancy and excitement of exploring the local past on its own terms.

Maynooth Studies in Local History: Number 111

The Easter Rising of 1916 in north County Dublin: a Skerries perspective

Peter F. Whearity

FOUR COURTS PRESS

Leabharlanna Cabrai
Cabra Library
Tel: 8691414

Set in 10pt on 12pt Bembo by
Carrigboy Typesetting Services for
FOUR COURTS PRESS LTD
7 Malpas Street, Dublin 8, Ireland
www.fourcourtspress.ie
and in North America for
FOUR COURTS PRESS
c/o ISBS, 920 N.E. 58th Avenue, Suite 300, Portland, OR 97213.

© Peter F. Whearity and Four Courts Press 2013

ISBN 978–1–84682–402–9

All rights reserved. Without limiting the rights
under copyright reserved alone, no part of this
publication may be reproduced, stored in or intro-
duced into a retrieval system, or transmitted, in any
form or by any means (electronic, mechanical,
photocopying, recording or otherwise), without the
prior written permission of both the copyright
owner and the above publisher of this book.

Printed in Ireland
by SprintPrint, Dublin.

Contents

	Acknowledgments	6
	Introduction	7
1	A brief preamble to the 1916 Rising	10
2	The 1916 Rising in north Co. Dublin	20
3	The battle of Ashbourne	30
4	After Pearse surrendered	40
	Conclusion	55
	APPENDIX: list of names of 114 men arrested after the Rising	58
	Notes	60

FIGURES

1	Map of north Co. Dublin	8
2	Thomas Ashe, commandant, Fifth Battalion 1916	11
3	Hamilton monument, Strand Street, Skerries	13
4	Skerries National Volunteers on parade, August 1914	16
5	Newbarn camp sheds (c.2004)	37
6	Memorial at Rath Cross, Ashbourne, Co. Meath	38
7	Places where north Co. Dublin men were interned	41
8	Volleys over Thomas Ashe's grave	53

TABLES

1	Irish Volunteer companies formed up to 11 June 1914	15
2	National Volunteer companies at end August 1914	17
3	National Volunteer companies at the Redmondite-split	18
4	Sixteen places from which arrested men came	41
5	Category 'A' prisoners from north Co. Dublin	43
6	Category 'B' prisoners	45
7	Category 'C' prisoners	46
8	Classification of arrested men on RIC and DMP lists, 1916	47

Acknowledgments

There are many people to whom I owe thanks for my having arrived at the happy place with the MA in Local History at NUI Maynooth completed, and now having that work feature as a Maynooth local history volume. In the first instance my gratitude goes to Prof. R.V. Comerford, who supervised my BA thesis and then encouraged my entry to the MA course. To my MA thesis supervisor, Prof. Terence Dooley, whose expert guidance brought me successfully through the thesis modules in good order. To Prof. Raymond Gillespie, course director of the MA in local history, for his invitation to have my work appear as one of his Maynooth local studies volumes. Thanks also go to other lecturers on the course, Denis Cronin and Rob Goodbody. Thanks to the staff of the John Paul II Library, NUI Maynooth. Also the staff of Fingal Co. Council Library and Local Studies Archive, Swords, for permission to use photographs. Likewise, to the editor of the *Meath Chronicle*. The Skerries public library staff were always helpful. To Conor Dineen (MA), for making a fine map of north Co. Dublin, specifically for this study. Thanks to Dr Maighréad Ní Mhurchadha, Skerries, for her enduring encouragement and mentoring throughout my study period. It was Dr Joseph Byrne's certificate course in local history at Pobal Scoil Íosa, Malahide, that provided the catalyst for me to enter further study under the auspices of the Department of Adult Education, under Josephine Finn. Thanks also to Lillie and Thomas Derham, and Teresa McCann, Skerries, for use of their relatives' papers. The Skerries, Balbriggan, and Loughshinny-Rush, historical societies were also helpful. Maree Baker made past papers available on request and Joe Murray supplied photographs. Thanks to my wife Valerie, and Helen, Colin, Derek, Emily, Rachel and Abi. This work is dedicated to my parents, Mary and the late James (Jim).

Introduction

This story is about the Irish Volunteers of north Co. Dublin, in the period before, during, and after the Easter Rising of 1916. However, the story will be told from the perspective of the Skerries Company of Irish Volunteers. To do so, all the companies in the above-mentioned area will need to be examined. When it comes to delineating the geographical area of north Dublin, it can be said that there were only four boundaries to consider. One of these, the southern boundary, was the most problematic as it was prone to encroachment from the conurbation of Dublin City into the rural area to its north. To begin with, there were a number of townships, namely Clontarf, Drumcondra, Clonliffe, Glasnevin and Chapelizod, which had already been built on former north Co. Dublin land.[1] Therefore, from the map (see fig. 1), it will be seen that a line is drawn from Raheny on the coast, which skirts around the township's northern fringes, but takes into the study area the villages of Artane, Santry, Finglas, Castleknock and Ashtown. It then follows the River Liffey, up-stream to a point beyond Blanchardstown, where the counties of Dublin, Meath and Kildare meet, and that should satisfactorily define the southern boundary for our purposes. The northern boundary was delineated by the course of the River Delvin, from its confluence with the Irish Sea, up-stream to the village of Naul where it ended. The eastern boundary is relatively easily defined by the coastal fringe of the Irish Sea, and it will be seen from the map that there were a number of small estuaries and peninsulas along its relatively low-lying length. The western boundary is problematical, as it meanders over an area which has no clear topographical feature to help define it. Former Oldtown resident and schoolteacher Patrick Archer wrote that 'The western boundary is left undefined for a distance of some thirteen miles … it extends southwards to a point on the northern bank of the River Tolka somewhere between Cardiff's bridge (near Finglas), and Blanchardstown'.[2] North Co. Dublin is relatively flat, apart from a range of low hills situated in the north-west corner near Naul, and lesser hills at Howth and Lambay Island. The tallest is the hill of Knockbrack at 176 metres high.[3] The towns and villages of the area had long been situated in the baronies of Balrothery (east and west), Coolock, a portion of Castleknock, and Nethercross.[4] A baronial map of Co. Dublin, c.1655, shows this to good effect.[5] The main population centres in c.1911: Balbriggan (2,273), Donabate (2,503), Swords (1,893), Skerries (1,819), and the combined parish of Lusk and Rush (1,304).[6]

Leabharlanna Poiblí Chathair Bhaile Átha Cliath
Dublin City Public Libraries

1 Map of north Co. Dublin and adjacent part of Co. Meath
(by Conor Dinneen, Skerries).

The historiography of the Irish Volunteer movement nationally is rather complex, and that was also the case in north Co. Dublin. Of particular significance for this work is a volume published by Fingal Co. Council Library and Local Studies Archive in 2010, and titled *Fingal Studies*, No. 1, on the theme of 'Fingal at war'. Three articles which provided valuable information were, Bernard Howard, 'The British Army and Fingal during the Great War'; Bairbre Curtis, 'Fingal and the Easter Rising 1916'; and Peter Whearity, 'John Jack "Rover" McCann (1886–1920): Irish Volunteer'.[7] The source known as the Bureau of Military History Witness Statements is important and now more accessible online. Fearghal McGarry has written that while information about well-known figures are found there, it also contains details which provide insights into the experiences of 'lesser-known political activists, individuals who never became household names, but were crucial to the success of the republican movement'.[8] Many of those who feature in this story fall into the latter category.

The questions expected to arise here might include 'when and where in north Co. Dublin did Irish Volunteer companies form?' 'What occurred during the change-over from being Irish Volunteers under Eoin MacNeill, to being National Volunteers under John Redmond, MP and the Irish Parliamentary Party?' 'How representative were the north Co. Dublin Volunteers in the so-called Howth gun-running, and what, if any, arms were obtained by them?' 'How did the Redmondite-split affect the Volunteer companies in the area in the autumn of 1914, and how many followed MacNeill or Redmond?' 'At the time of the 1916 Rising, how many mobilized with the Fifth Battalion under Commandant Thomas Ashe?' 'What happened during the Rising itself, particularly during the event known as the battle of Ashbourne?' 'What was the aftermath of the Rising, with regard to those who participated in it?' 'How involved were the Volunteers of Skerries in that dramatic and interesting historical episode in Irish history?' While it is relatively easy to ask questions, it is another matter when trying to answer them, but in this case, fortunately, the sources were both abundant and readily accessible.

The approach used here is to study the Volunteers as a 'community of interest', that in essence is any group of like-minded individuals acting together in pursuit of a common goal. While bearing in mind the important concepts of 'people, place and time', with the greatest emphasis being on the people involved, then this is a pragmatic way of studying groups such as the Irish Volunteers.[9] Bulmer Hobson hinted at this in his 1909 work, *Defensive warfare: a handbook for Irish Nationalists*, when he stated that a 'community of national sentiment will go so far, but a community of interest to back it up will be stronger still'.[10] The first objective is to identify the people involved and then to profile them. Considerations of space preclude detailed tables on which the quantitative analysis is based. While a list of names of those arrested after the Rising will feature, the associated details such as occupations, ages, martial status and so on will not.[11]

1. A brief preamble to the 1916 Rising

The idea behind the formation of the Irish Volunteer movement came from Eoin MacNeill, then vice-president of the Gaelic League, whose thoughts on the matter were published in an editorial titled 'How the North began' in *An Claideamh Soluis*, on 1 November 1913. Therein he raised the possibility that home-rulers should follow the northern Unionist's template of the Ulster Volunteer Force (UVF), and replicate it in the south.[1] MacNeill's membership of the Gaelic League was important and R.V. Comerford points out that 'a majority of the signatories of the proclamation of the Irish Republic on Easter Monday 1916 had been activists in the literary or language revivals, or both'.[2] A public meeting at the Rotunda Hall, Dublin, on 25 November, saw the Irish Volunteer movement established. Its aims and aspirations, such as they were, appeared in the December 1913 issue of the *Volunteer Gazette*.[3] Prominent figures behind it included Patrick Pearse, Michael Davitt, Sean T. O'Kelly, James MacMahon, Michael J. Judge, Sean Mac Diarmada and Bulmer Hobson. Two north Co. Dublin brothers, Thomas and Laurence Kettle, participated at the inaugural meeting: Thomas helped MacNeill with editing the manifesto and Laurence read the document in the Rotunda Hall, all the while having to endure protestors repeatedly shouting 'up (James), Larkin'. Despite the din created, afterwards about 4,000 men enrolled as Irish Volunteers.[4]

Among those who welcomed the new Volunteer organization was Richard Mulcahy, who was born in Waterford in 1886, and came to Dublin in 1907, where he joined the Teeling circle of the Irish Republican Brotherhood (IRB). He also joined the Keating branch of the Gaelic League, where he rubbed shoulders with Michael Collins and Cathal Brugha.[5]

Bulmer Hobson thought that 'the Irish Volunteer movement was the spontaneous creation of the Irish people themselves … (However), the political leaders who had secured the adhesion of the great majority of the people of Ireland not only took no part in its inception, but were and remained definitely hostile to it'. MacNeill added that 'Mr Redmond, in the early period of the Irish Volunteer organization was content or had to content himself with the English attitude. He did what he could to discourage the Volunteer movement and to dissuade his supporters from joining it'.[6]

An influential figure in the Volunteer movement in north Co. Dublin was Thomas Ashe, who was born on a farm at Lispole, Co. Kerry, in 1885 (fig. 2). He was brought up in the Irish musical traditions and was fluent in the Irish language. On completion of his education at the De la Salle training college,

2 Thomas Ashe (by courtesy of Fingal Co. Council Library and
Local Studies Archive, Swords).

Waterford, in 1907, he took up a post as a schoolteacher at Corduff national
school, Lusk.[7] He soon became 'indelibly linked to this area because of his
subsequent political, military, musical and cultural activities' and his stay there
was to last eight years, albeit seven months were spent funding-raising in the
United States for the Gaelic League.[8] Among the several Gaelic League
branches in north Co. Dublin, one at Balcunnin, Skerries, was founded c.1901.
On a committee elected in December 1904 was its vice-president was Thomas
Hand.[9] Hand was employed as a van-man who sold bread in his own locale.
He was a local representative for the Irish Transport and General Workers
Union, and secretary of the Skerries Dr Grimley, No. 414, branch of the Irish
National Foresters for the years 1912 to c.1918. His membership of the Irish
Volunteers extended from its inception in 1913, until he was killed in
December 1920 by the auxiliary police force known as the 'Black and Tans'.
He is mentioned by Sean O Mahony in *Frongoch: university of revolution.*[10]

In May 1914, the County Inspector, Reginald Heard, reported that until
then the Irish Volunteers had progressed only slowly in north Co. Dublin.

However, the four branches that he knew about were at Swords, Clondalkin, Lusk and Skerries. That at Swords had formed about a month earlier, while the Skerries Company (after an initial earlier meeting to gauge what interest was there) was formed on 24 May. He nevertheless felt that while the movement was in its infancy, it was drawn from the lower social classes with only labourers and small farmers and their sons being part of it. In addition, the Catholic clergy were withholding their support, at least for the present. Despite these limitations the Volunteers were persisting with exercises and marching and new members were still enrolling. While he believed that men of prominence would stay away from it, he foresaw two more companies being formed at Rush and Garristown, in the near future.[11] The company formed at Swords on 6 April 1914 was designated as the headquarters of the movement in north Co. Dublin.[12]

It is possible, or even probable, that the later formation at Skerries had to do with a poor landlord-tenant relationship there. The antagonism was between the proprietor of the town, Lord Holmpatrick, his land-agent George Fowler (the former lived near Castleknock, Co. Dublin, while the latter lived at Kells, Co. Meath) and the town-tenants on the Holmpatrick estate in Skerries. Many attempts were made to calm the waters there, but even the intervention of William Field, MP, in January and February 1914 failed to extinguish the rancour between the interested parties. The trouble had to do with demands for rent reductions, the sale of the town to the tenants, the purchase price and the ability or willingness of the tenants to pay that price.[13] It boiled down to the fact that the landlord wanted more than the tenants could, or would, pay.

Schoolteacher Paddy Sexton wrote that 'one of the best landmarks in Skerries was the obelisk or monument in the main (Strand) street' (see fig. 3). From the website of the Skerries Historical Society 'overview of Skerries history, part two', is found the following details of the inscription on the monument:

> This monument was erected in memory of James Hans Hamilton, Esq. M.P. Abbotstown House, Co. Dublin by the tenantry of his several estates viz.: Holmpatrick, Dublin, Meath, Carlow, Down and Queen's County in testimony of their esteem for him as a kind friend and benevolent landlord. He represented this county in parliament for twenty-two years and died 19th June 1863.[14]

Whatever about the words on the inscription about this Lord Holmpatrick there are several accounts that paint the Lord Holmpatrick who was living in the period of interest here in a poor light as a landlord. David Patrick (D.P.) Moran, proprietor of the *Leader*, a Dublin newspaper, in an article titled 'Merry Skerries', in September 1911, wrote that 'Holmpatrick owns the whole town,

3 Hamilton monument, c.early 20th century, Strand Street, Skerries (by courtesy of
Joe Murray, Hon. Archivist, Skerries Historical Society).

but did little for it except draw rents'. He has 'not put one brick on top of
another up till then. When leases expire the landlord raises the rent and as he
owns the whole place he therefore can squeeze the people there very tightly'.[15]

The Volunteer companies in north Co. Dublin, when compared with those
in the metropolitan area (examples being at Clontarf and Drumcondra, which
formed on 1 December 1913), could be said to have been somewhat lethargic
in their formation.[16] However, that appeared to have been the case in other
rural areas throughout the country, albeit there were a few exceptions found,
as at Athboy, Co. Meath, where a company formed on 17 March, and another
formed at Dundalk, Co. Louth, on 22 February 1914.[17] It was in that
environment that two local men had been successful in establishing a company
of Volunteers at Skerries. The first was Patrick Mathews, a 46-year-old married
man, a foreman stone-cutter at Milverton quarry, situated on the outskirts of
Skerries. He was also a town-tenant, and secretary of the Skerries town-tenant
committee to boot. The second man, Patrick O'Driscoll, was a local insurance
broker and probably also a town-tenant. He was born in Co. Cork and was

49 years old, with a family, and married to a Canadian woman. Before coming to Skerries to live and work, he had spent a period of his life in New South Wales. Before settling in Skerries, he was a member of the United Irish League, and on occasion acted as chairman of the north Dublin United Irish League Executive (UIL). He was a supporter of the policies of John Redmond's Irish Parliamentary Party.[18] Because of his past history, and his knowledge of the wider world, he could be seen as an outside-broker for change within the more locally based community of Skerries, but for all that, his political views differed little from those espoused by Mathews, who lived all his life there.

Following an earlier public meeting held on 10 May, to test the feelings of the town's inhabitants for having an Irish Volunteer Company formed, a second public meeting was held on Sunday 24 May (Empire day), at the Square, close to the Holmpatrick monument. It attracted some 300 people and P.J. O'Driscoll presided and spoke at the event where he lambasted the 'jelly-fish government' for not having prevented the UVF from becoming an armed force. Other men, who spoke in favour of forming a company at Skerries, were L.J. Kettle, who told the gathering that the Volunteer movement was essentially a movement not of oratory but of action. 'The voice of this movement was the tramp of marching men and the crack of rifles … Yet the Volunteers were not formed in any aggressive spirit, they were essentially an army of national defence'. Other speakers were Patrick J. Kettle, J.P. Swords, and James Glennon, a local publican and grocer. While Patrick Mathews and J. Boylan from Skerries attended, regrets came from the Revd R. Smyth, CC, and Michael Dunne, JP, who was a member of Dublin County Council. In a telegram, John J. Clancy, MP, then in the house of commons awaiting the passage of the third stage of the home rule bill, regretted his non-attendance but wrote that he 'admired the spirit shown and wished the Skerries men great success'. Afterwards some 200 men enrolled in the new company.[19]

While Volunteer companies were being established countrywide, there was, in late April 1914, a paucity of arms to drill with. This resulted in Volunteers in the south of Ireland having to use wooden arms or sticks, at a time when the UVF under Edward Carson were importing up to 25,000 arms and ammunition at Larne, Belfast, and other places along the northern coastline.[20] Not only was the UVF growing in strength, but the so-called Curragh mutiny incident saw 60 cavalry officers defy the government's order to 'coerce Ulster Unionists into accepting home rule' and got away with it.[21] Around then, plans were being put in place by northern unionist James Craig for the evacuation of Ulster women and children to places of safety and hospitality in England in the event that civil war was to break out in Ireland.[22] In the south of Ireland, the Volunteer movement gathered momentum until early June, when it was subsumed by John Redmond's Irish Parliamentary Party, whence it became known as the 'National Volunteers'. David Fitzpatrick has suggested that until then the UIL and the Irish Parliamentary Party were 'suspicious and resentful of the movement's success', but that ultimately its 'vampire urge prevailed'.[23] On 11 June, a statement was issued by the Irish Volunteer's Provisional Committee's joint-secretaries, Eoin MacNeill and L.J. Kettle, who reluctantly accepted Redmond as the movement's new leader.[24] This date has been chosen for the purposes of this account as being a suitable time whereby the two movements became as one. In table 1, it can be seen that at the time of the take-over, in numerical terms, the Skerries Irish Volunteer Company was the largest by far, even when the lowest estimated figure is used for the calculation.

Table 1. Irish Volunteer companies formed up to 11 June 1914[25]

	Company name	No. members	Company formation date
1	Swords	50–55	Monday 6 Apr. (all 1914)
2	Balbriggan	5	Sunday 4 May
3	Lusk	40	Tuesday 19 May
4	Skerries	105–200	Sunday 24 May
5	Garristown	No details	Before 3 June
6	Santry	No details	Before 10 June

Total No. members (200), or, if the higher estimates are used (300).

In order to get arms, the so-called Howth gun-running took place on Sunday 26 July, when some 1,000 National Volunteers from Dublin City and another 250 from north Co. Dublin participated in successfully landing much-needed arms. The Volunteers of Skerries, some 70 to 80 strong, joined others from Lusk, Swords, St Margaret's and Donabate at the rendezvous point at Raheny, before joining the main column for the march to Howth. Bernard McAllister saw a contingent from Rush at the seaside village and witnessed Skerries man, Matt Derham getting a rifle on the pier.[26] The already mentioned Thomas Hand was also part of the Skerries contingent.[27] The *Times* stated that 'the guns were packed in straw and in a very brief time each of the volunteers possessed a rifle. The others were put on motorcars and whisked away to various parts of the country. Some of them it is said were taken as far as Skerries'.[28] The county inspector stated that 'on Sunday, 26 July, gun-running was carried out on an extensive scale at Howth. A large body of Volunteers, numbering about 1,200, marched into Howth at 12.45 p.m. and took possession of the east pier'. Among the group from the county area were L.J. Kettle and Michael Dunne and they played an important part in the proceedings. At the entrance to the pier four companies took up position and oversaw the speedy unloading of arms onto the pier and thence into waiting arms. While the on-looking RIC estimated that some 864 rifles were quickly

4 Volunteers on parade at Skerries in August 1914 (courtesy of Joe Murray, Skerries Historical Society).

removed from the pier, it later transpired that the county inspector was satisfied that 1,000 were landed. The bulk of the rifles went to the Dublin contingents, but the inspector recorded that of the '54 rifles given to members in the Co. Dublin district (50 to Skerries branch, 2 to Howth and 2 to Swords)'.[29] It is remarkable that the Skerries contingent should get such a haul of arms while other contingents got few or none at all. The arms came from the sailing yacht *Asgard*, piloted by Erskine Childers, his wife Molly, and Mary Spring-Rice. Other estimates of the quantity of arms taken ashore vary; Diarmaid Ferriter suggests that 1,500 rifles were landed.[30]

On the return journey to Dublin, there were clashes between Volunteers, police and soldiers at different places along the route. The most serious incident occurred at Batchelor's Walk, Dublin, where at least three civilians were killed by mounted cavalry returning to barracks. The events at Howth and Batchelor's Walk were subsequently investigated by a Royal Commission of inquiry in August 1914, at Dublin's Four Courts. As part of his statement, the county inspector said that the 250 Volunteers from the county should be watched and a record kept of where they went. However, when giving his evidence at the courts, the only Volunteer group named by him was that from Skerries.[31] With regard to the rifles brought home to Skerries, a resident of there, Paddy Halpin, remembered Volunteers parading in the town in August 1914, where he said that 'all were agog with their new toy, the German Mauser rifle' (see fig. 4).[32]

On the same day as the Howth gun-running, a large number of national Volunteers had gone to Naul to help form a company there. On the day itself, some 150 men from Balbriggan, headed by St Patrick's Brass band, left for the one-hour march to Naul. When all the Volunteer contingents arrived there, with 200 from Co. Meath companies at Stamullen and Julianstown, 50 from Gormanstown, along with 80 thought to have been from Balrothery, they collectively numbered some 480 men. The 140 who enrolled at Naul are not included in the above figure. An important aspect was the cross-county interaction between Volunteer companies seen in that district, and which also included combined route marches and drill exercises.[33]

The first days of August saw the outbreak of the First World War. While the ramifications for Europe were immense, for Ireland too there were serious consequences. Perhaps the most important of these was the shelving of the home rule bill, which had promised much, and was heavily supported by John Redmond and the Irish Parliamentary Party. Other aspects related to the possibility of forced conscription into the British army, and the call-up of former National Volunteer drill instructors to join the war effort. The loss of

Table 2. Number of National Volunteer companies prior to end of Aug. 1914[34]

(Included are those former Irish Volunteer companies from table 1)

	Company name	No. members	Company formation date 1914
1	Swords	50–55	Monday 6 Apr. (all 1914)
2	Balbriggan	200–350	Prior to 8 Aug.
3	Lusk	40–80	Tuesday 19 May
4	Skerries	105–200	Sunday 24 May
5	Garristown	No details	Before 3 June
6	Santry	No details	Before 10 June
7	Coolock	No details	Before 13 June
8	Donabate	No details	Sunday 21 June
9	St Margaret's	No details	Sunday 5 July
10	Blanchardstown	200	Before 12 July
11	Balrothery	50	Before 25 July
12	Howth	No details	Before 26 July
13	Naul	140–150	19 July
14	Balscadden	No details	Before 28 July
15	Rush	100–250	Sunday 2 Aug.
16	Malahide	No details	Saturday 15 Aug.

Total No. Volunteers, using highest figures, 1,335

Table 3. National Volunteer companies at the Redmondite-split[35]

No.	Company name	Date of split (all 1914)	Other details
1	Swords	28 Aug.	75 for Redmond, 15 for MacNeill
2	Balbriggan	28 Sept.	All for Redmond
3	Lusk	30 Sept.	Majority for Redmond
4	St Margaret's	Sept.	No details
5	Raheny	Before 3 Oct.	All for Redmond
6	Santry	Before 3 Oct.	Majority for Redmond
7	Rush	Before 3 Oct.	All for Redmond
8	Garristown	11 Oct.	All for Redmond
9	Naul	17 Oct.	All for Redmond
10	Baldoyle	No details	Collapsed in Oct.
11	Skerries	23 Oct.	60 for Redmond, 31 for MacNeill, 2 neutral

the latter was a setback to Volunteer companies wherever they occurred. Several from north Co. Dublin had gone by August, and when James Gosson, the Skerries Volunteer company instructor, left on 12 August, over 100 members turned out to wish adieu to the man who led them at Howth, and helped them claim their rifles.[36] Bairbre Curtis adds that the Skerries Company's Captain, Joseph McGuinness was also involved there.[37] Nevertheless, companies continued to form in north Co. Dublin, and table 2 shows what the situation was then. However, table 2 is understated numerically because of a lack of enrolment details for half the companies on the list.

    John Redmond was supportive of the British war effort from the start, but as he became more vociferous in that regard he began to cause discontent among the former Irish Volunteer element within the National Volunteers. Michael McAllister felt that Redmond had turned his party 'into recruiting agents for the British army'.[38] Redmond, when speaking at Woodenbridge, Co. Wicklow, on 20 September 1914, said 'I am glad to see such magnificent material for soldiers around me, and I say to you; go on drilling and make yourselves efficient for the work … not only in Ireland itself, but wherever the firing extends in defence of rights of freedom and religion in this war'.[39] That, and other speeches Redmond gave, led to the Volunteer movement breaking into two factions, one under Redmond and another under MacNeill. The event became known as the Redmondite-split. Table 3 provides details of how the break-up wreaked havoc on companies in north Co. Dublin. The Skerries Company was the last to split, but it was amicable in that it was agreed that 'should a spirit of rivalry exist, it would be a healthy one and in no way encourage local bitterness'.[40] Nationally, according to F.X. Martin, some 181,000 Volunteers remained loyal to Redmond, as National Volunteers, while about 11,000 reverted to MacNeill's control as Irish Volunteers.[41]

In January 1915, Piaras Beaslaí believed that Thomas Ashe was 'already the leading spirit of the Fifth, or Fingal Battalion'.[42] Richard Mulcahy, on the other hand, pointed out that prior to Ashe's prominence there had already been a strong leadership in north Co. Dublin in the guise of Frank Lawless and Dr Richard Hayes.[43] In any case, the Volunteers (of both factions) in the area were then preoccupied with manoeuvres, first-aid, intelligence gathering, signalling and other useful military skills.[44] Hayes recorded that the Volunteers of north Co. Dublin were more often known as the Sinn Féin Volunteers. In the middle of 1915 the Fifth Battalion numbered less than 100 and more usually was about 80. They underwent rifle practice, small-scale manoeuvres and also received lectures from Eimar O'Duffy, who had earlier received training at the (Royal), Military Academy, Sandhurst, Surrey, England.[45] Christopher Moran recorded that there was a battalion in operation around that time consisting of small companies at Lusk, Turvey, St Margaret's, Cloghran and Skerries. A member of its governing committee was Joseph Derham, Skerries.[46]

In 1915, the death in America of former Fenian, Jeremiah O'Donovan Rossa, was of great importance to the Irish Volunteer movement in Ireland. His funeral procession in August of that year drew thousands to line the route to Glasnevin cemetery, Dublin. The participation of the National Volunteers was the first time since the 'Redmondite-split' that both Volunteer factions had attended the same event together, but their differences were put aside out of respect for Rossa.[47] It seemed that the 'Irish Party remained proud of its Fenian antecedents and had for decades praised a long succession of rebels and martyrs to the cause [of Irish freedom]'.[48]

2. The 1916 Rising in north Co. Dublin

The Dublin Castle authorities stated in their intelligence notes that in 1916 Co. Dublin began peaceably. However, there were concerns about anti-British sentiment in some quarters there. It was thought that while Irish Volunteer numbers were then low, that, nonetheless, they influenced the labourers and shop boys, and attracted their loyalties.[1] On the whole, apart from a Sinn Féin element, the people there were 'a law abiding lot, who were on good terms with the police'. The county inspector recorded in his March 1916 confidential report, that the National Volunteers 'exist only in name' while the Irish Volunteers were of 'very little account' … with only four companies at Rathfarnham, Swords, Lusk and Balbriggan, with a combined membership of 186 men.[2] There was no reference made to the Skerries Company then very much in existence, but no reason can be ascribed to its omission. Joseph Lawless recorded that:

> Prior to the Rising of 1916 the Volunteers in Fingal were organized as the Fifth Battalion of the Dublin Brigade, and consisted of four companies located at Swords, Lusk, Skerries and St Margarets', each with a nominal roll of about thirty men. Some weeks before the Rising, the command of the battalion was assumed by Commandant Thomas Ashe, in succession to Doctor R. Hayes, who became battalion adjutant. The position of the battalion quartermaster was held … by Frank Lawless.[3]

In the latter part of 1915, the company captains were (and presumably still were in early 1916) Richard Coleman, Swords; Edward Rooney, Lusk; Joseph Thornton, Skerries and James V. Lawless, St Margaret's. The Volunteers of Donabate were (loosely) attached to the Swords Company.[4] Frank Lawless, as quartermaster, with his son Joseph, went to Kimmage, Co. Dublin, on Good Friday to get military supplies ostensibly for use in the Rising. Among the goods were 20 single-barrelled shotguns, buckshot, 60 pounds of gelignite, detonators and fuses, and field dressings, which they brought back to their farm at Saucerstown, near Swords.[5] It is likely that the war materials were obtained at the Larkfield home of Joseph Mary Plunkett's mother. That place was used as a base for the manufacture of explosives, for storing weapons and as a training ground and place of refuge for Irish Volunteers from abroad.[6] Ann Mathews gives an account of the several hundred Irish Volunteers from Glasgow, Liverpool, and London, who came to Dublin to participate in the

Rising. A large number of them stayed at the Larkfield Mill.[7] Regarding the medical field dressings, Nancy Wyse-Power and a coterie of women were making iodine and bandage packages in late 1915 and early 1916, ostensibly for use by the north Co. Dublin, and presumably other, Volunteer companies in the Dublin region. A batch was made ready for Frank Lawless to collect on Easter Saturday morning from Wyse-Power's home at 3 Wellington Place. The goods were made at 2 Dawson Street, the headquarters of the Irish Volunteers in Dublin.[8]

In the first week of April 1916, Thomas Ashe had a close relationship with James Connolly and was also 'much in touch with the Irish Republican Brotherhood (IRB) Supreme Council'. Ashe was officially informed, verbally, by Connolly that the Rising was fixed to start on Easter Sunday at 7 p.m. and that the news could be shared with Frank Lawless and Dick Hayes.[9] However, as is well known, the plans were scuppered by order of Eoin MacNeill, then president of the Volunteer Executive Council. His statement directed that:

> Owing to the very critical position, all orders given to Irish Volunteers for tomorrow Easter Sunday, are hereby rescinded and no parades, marches, or other movements of Irish Volunteers will take place. Each Volunteer will obey this order strictly in every particular.[10]

While the order reached the Dublin companies in time for them to abort their plans that was not necessarily the case elsewhere. The news came too late for the Fifth Battalion, and its members turned out 120 strong, on Easter Sunday, at Rathbeale Cross, Swords. Charles Weston, who gave the above estimate, also recorded that the largest contingent was from Skerries.[11] Reports of the number of those who mobilized varies, with some sources estimating that up to 200 men turned out there.[12] To clarify matters, Joseph Lawless brought a message from Ashe to James Connolly, then at Liberty Hall, Dublin. He returned later with news 'that all was off for the moment, but to hold in readiness to act at any time'. Around midnight, the Fifth Battalion men were sent home, with the order to 'guard your arms as you would guard your lives, you never know the moment you may be called upon to use them'.[13] However, on the next morning, a message from Patrick Pearse reached Ashe, with the order to 'strike at one o'clock today'. Ashe made arrangements for a second mobilization point at Knocksedan bridge, Swords (see fig. 1).[14] As time went along, it became apparent that the turnout would be much less than the previous day. In the event, only about 60 men had returned, and among those absent were the men from Skerries.[15] Such a poor turnout was not an aberration, and Ernie O'Malley estimated that of the nearly 3,000 who mobilized countrywide on the Easter Sunday, the number had effectively halved on the next day, Monday.[16] Frank Robbins, then an active Irish

Volunteer in Dublin city, wrote that the order by MacNeill 'caused a tremendous shortage of men for various positions'.[17]

On Easter Monday, the Rising began in Dublin's Sackville (later to become O'Connell) Street with the take-over of the General Post Office (GPO) by James Connolly's Irish Citizen Army and a band of Irish Volunteers. At midday, Pearse, acting as commandant-genera (commander in chief) of the army of the Irish Republic and president of the provisional government, read the Proclamation and declared to the world that Ireland was from that moment a Republic.[18] Connolly had responsibility for the Volunteers in the Dublin districts, and declared that 'communications with the country is largely cut, but reports to hand show that the country is Rising. Bodies of men from Kildare and Fingal have already reported in Dublin'.[19]

The absence of the Skerries men on the second mobilization is partly explained by a hand-written note by Matt Derham. He wrote for the benefit of his family, the following story:

> Easter week 1916: Seamus (James McDonnell), Terry (Sherlock), Tom Hand; Jem Kelly; Pete Gibbons; Jack McGowan and Joe Thornton. Mobilized Easter Sunday at 4.30 at Crossroads, Rathbeale, Saucerstown, Swords, with amassed Fingal Brigade (it was a battalion in 1916), was on duty until 10.30 withdrew to Mr Frank Lawless' yard and dismissed at 12.30 (a.m.), and sent home. Monday, got garbled accounts of the happenings in the city, but nothing definite until some residents of there, returning by the last train, told me about the post office (GPO) being occupied, went round to the Volunteer who had rifles and ammunition. The railway arch at Skerries, the only direct exit from the town, was then already guarded from the evening. However, I got the boys who had rifles and we succeeded in running the guards for the rifles and ammunition on the country side of the railway, stored in an old farmhouse. We were told by the country people that there was no possibility of going the roads in the area as any person crossing had been held up by the military and police. We decided to send on scouts without arms in two directions to locate the brigade, as they were supposed to be about Killeek, or Santry. The scouts got in touch with the Volunteers but did not return, but on the Tuesday afternoon I received a message to hold on in Skerries until Wednesday, as the brigade were coming to attack the military wireless station at Skerries. Wednesday, received a message that the attack on the wireless (station), was off, that the brigade (battalion), went west to Garristown. Under cover of evening I got out of Skerries and proceeded to form up with the remaining Volunteers and arranged to go singly and meet at Kileek next morning. Four of us met there and could not find the brigade or

any trace of them. We cycled for hours without getting in touch and decided to go into the city and see if we could get in touch with the city forces. We were held up at the metal bridge in Drumcondra, so we detoured down Clonliffe Road to the North Strand. We got held up there by soldiers and retreated back to the metal bridge and as curfew was on, we left the city again and cycled through Fingal, without getting in touch with the Volunteers. We went through Oldtown, Ballyboughal, Garristown, and towards evening we met a man, an overseer on the roads who told us that there was fighting going on in the direction of Ashbourne, we proceeded hence, only to get in touch with the Volunteers, after the fight (the battle of Ashbourne), was over. We camped that night, next morning broke camp and proceeded in a body to a new base camp. On Saturday night fearing an attack on camp, took up duty on the outskirts of the farmyard until recalled at dawn. We got the order to surrender from headquarters, which order was verified by a messenger going into the city on a motorcycle sidecar. We were rounded up on Monday evening by the military, taken into Swords, and taken by lorry to Richmond barracks. With many others I was deported on 2 May, to Knutsford prison, hence to Frongoch, released at the end of July.

Signed, Matthias Derham, 72 Church Street, Skerries. Address in 1916, Hoar Rock, Skerries.[20]

Much of the above is self-explanatory, but some clarification is needed. Did the order to remobilize actually reach Skerries? From Derham's account it seems unlikely as otherwise he would not have needed to frequent the Skerries railway station looking for news. From Joseph Lawless' account, while mentioning spreading the word, he made no mention about going to Skerries. His priority, in his own words, was to recall 'key men' such as Ned Rooney, Lusk; the Westons and the McAllisters, Turvey; the Taylors, Swords; Jim Lawless, Cloghran and Tom Dukes at St Margaret's.[21] Derham stated in his note that scouts had gone from Skerries to locate Ashe's unit, and though they did so, they did not return. Therefore, given the likelihood that the scouts went off in pairs rather than singly, then at best, two, or possibly four, had joined the Fifth Battalion on the Monday night or the Tuesday morning. Paul O'Brien pointed out that on the Wednesday morning, James Kelly, Peter Ganly and Jack McGowan had arrived into Ashe's camp at Finglas. McGowan was sent away because he was too young, while the others were appointed to sections within the battalion.[22] In Anne Clare's work, after having spoken to Paddy Halpin at Skerries, it is suggested that McGowan was sent home to incapacitate the Marconi wireless station.[23] It seems unlikely, however, that a youth considered too young to fight with the Fifth Battalion, would be asked to undertake such an action on his own. It might have been the case that

McGowan concocted such a scenario to camouflage his disappointment at having been dismissed by Ashe. One of the two other Skerries men as mentioned above, whose name was Ganly, raises a problem in that other sources, including the *Sinn Fein rebellion handbook*, while giving the same address, give his name as Peter Gibbons.[24] Further research will be necessary to bring clarity to this matter which probably is a mix up between the Peter Gibbons adopted by the Ganlys in Argentina and his biological father whose name was also Peter Gibbons and lived beside the Ganlys near Skerries.

During Easter Week, Ashe and his small band followed James Connolly's order to create a diversion in north Co. Dublin. Seán Ó Luing put it succinctly in that 'Ashe led his men across the roads and fields of Fingal in an act of challenge to an empire'. He wrote that:

> In his small army were Fingal's best and bravest sons, the McAllisters of Turvey, their cousins the Westons, and their cousins, the Kellys; four Lawlesses shouldered their guns and marched; there were the Taylors and the Wilsons and the Doyles, who in the person of Paddy Doyle maintained the link with 1798; the Black Raven bandsmen were there; there was 19 year old Thomas Rafferty, who could not ordinarily join in the manoeuvres as his employment on the government farm at Lusk did not permit, but who promised to be there when the time came; there were Jack Crenigan and the Rover McCann, described by his comrade John McAllister as the bravest man a country ever had; Captain Richard Coleman led the Swords Company; there were men from Skerries and St Margaret's. Thirty turned up at Knocksedan, but many more joined during the day, until by evening there were between sixty and seventy men under Ashe's command.[25]

The connection between Paddy Doyle and the 1798 Rebellion is an interesting one. Peadar Bates points out that 'in the houses of Rorke, Russell and Doyle of Lusk, there were six wounded rebels who were wounded in the engagements in the County Wexford'.[26] Sean Ó Mahony provides details about Ashe at his new home at Corduff, near Lusk. It was there:

> His extracurricular activities once again came to the fore and he founded the Black Raven Pipe band in 1910. Ashe himself was a member of the band. It did extraordinarily well: the band won the Championship of Ireland at the Oireachtas in Galway in 1913, a mere three years after it was founded.[27]

James Connolly requested 40 men from Ashe's battalion so that city garrisons could be bolstered. Such a figure was out of the question if a viable force was to be maintained in north Co. Dublin and only half that number was sent away under the command of Richard (Dick) Coleman. This unavoidably left Ashe short-handed, but when a few Volunteer stragglers were accounted for, then a new estimate by Joseph Lawless put the figure at 45 men.[28] The new-comers had come on the Tuesday, including Patrick Grant, Thomas Maxwell, Richard Mulcahy and Jerry Golden.[29] Mulcahy and Ashe already knew each other from their participation in the Keating branch of the Gaelic League and a close-knit Irish Republican Brotherhood (IRB) circle in the city. Therefore, it was decided that Mulcahy would act as Ashe's second in command.[30] Because there were fewer men in the battalion, the tactics espoused by the 1911 British infantry training manual were deemed no longer applicable. Instead 'a scheme made to fit the numbers available and the tactical requirements of our mission' was devised and put into operation. Joseph Lawless viewed the new plan as 'quite sound from a tactical viewpoint'. The available man-power was separated into four sections, of 10 or 12 men each. An officer would be responsible for each section, and four other officers would act as a 'head-quarters and command staff'. The section at the back would act as a rear-guard and the middle, or main section, was to contain Ashe and officers acting as his staff. The sections would rotate duties as conditions demanded. Lawless felt that 'the commander and staff of the column [Ashe and Mulcahy] were a fortunate combination, and were largely, if not entirely, responsible for the successful exploits of the unit, including the Ashbourne battle'.[31] When it came to Ashe, Lawless saw him as a 'fine physical specimen of manhood, courageous, and high-principled. Something of a poet, painter and dreamer, he was perhaps in military matters somewhat unpractical'.[32]

An official interpretation of events in April 1916 comes from the RIC county inspector, who began by recording that, prior to Easter Sunday, Co. Dublin was peaceable. However, on the next day the Great Northern railway bridge at Rogerstown, situated on the line between Rush and Donabate, was damaged by explosives. The inspector is likely to have heard the explosion as he included in his confidential monthly report the words 'the conflagration had then commenced'.[33] The explosion at Rogerstown occurred at 2.30 p.m. and the quantity of explosives used was between 40 and 50 pounds of gelignite. The demolition party was led by Joseph Lawless, along with John Devine, Thomas Weston, John 'Rover' McCann, and John Hynes. It was McCann whose experience was crucial in setting the gelignite, fuses and detonators. Because the sea-level was high though, it meant that the explosive charges had to be placed near the top of the bridge rather than lower down on the main bridge supports. The result was that only minimal damage was caused to one set of rails. The damage was mainly to the down line. Compensation of £250 was later paid for the damaged bridge.[34]

The words used by the inspector to describe the event at Rogerstown are both interesting and open to interpretation, or miss-interpretation as the case might be. For a start, what area was he alluding to? Was it just that part of north Co. Dublin, located near his Howth office, or did he include the metropolitan area as well. From information about other bomb blasts, the *Sinn Féin rebellion handbook*, under the heading 'the storm breaks', is informative. On Easter Monday, it stated that the GPO and other important buildings in the city were taken over by Pearse's Irish Volunteers and Connolly's Irish Citizen Army, without encountering any serious resistance. The Magazine Fort in the Phoenix Park suffered a serious fire, but no report was made to the Central Fire Station at Tara Street until 3.58 p.m. When attempts were made by the rebels to damage rail lines and bridges at Blanchardstown and Cabra, these took place on the Monday night and Tuesday morning respectively.[35] Therefore, it might have been that the explosion at the Rogerstown rail bridge was the opening salvo, munitions wise, of the 1916 Rising, in Co. Dublin and perhaps the metropolitan area too. While the GPO was relatively easily taken over, it was recorded in the *Sinn Fein rebellion handbook* as 'the first act in this latest of Irish rebellions was performed'.[36]

The county inspector recorded in his April report, that on the Wednesday, the RIC barracks at Swords and Donabate was attacked at 2 a.m. and that at Garristown suffered a similar fate later. However, the latter barracks was practically empty as the police had already gone to Balbriggan barracks for security reasons, and had taken their arms with them. The inspector's view was that the rebels were from the Swords and Donabate districts, and their objective was to 'march to Howth to cut the cable to Holyhead'. Arrangements were quickly made by the inspector for the 20 military stationed there to be combined with his eight policemen in an attempt to ward off the expected raiding party. In the event, Howth was not attacked, and the inspector seemed convinced that it was the sight of 'two destroyers hurrying up the coast with troops from Kingstown to Skerries and Balbriggan' that caused the rebels to turn westward, and into the arms of the 'Meath police under [County Inspector Alexander] Gray'.[37]

The situation at Skerries was reported in the *Weekly Irish Times*, and the *Sinn Fein rebellion handbook*, under the headings 'Rebels foiled at Skerries' and 'Destroyers land troops at Skerries'. The story continued:

> Of the outlying portions of Co. Dublin affected by the late rising, Skerries had not the least exciting experience. On Easter Monday a war demonstration had been advertised, with Mr J[ohn] J. Clancy, KC, member for North Dublin, in the chair, and speakers from the Recruiting Department. When the occupants of the platform had taken their places word reached the local committee that the bridge at Donabate had been just blown up, that the train bringing the chairman and speakers was held up, and that the Sinn Féiners were out. Notwithstanding this grave news, it was decided not to alarm the

audience, but to hold the meeting. Mr Battersby, K[ing's] C[ouncil], was accordingly moved to the chair. Local speakers, Captain Taylor, Mr Fitzpatrick, and Mr Malone, with Lieutenant Clancy, took the place of the absentees, and certificates were given to the relatives of Skerries soldiers, one hundred in all, and the meeting passed off successfully.

On Tuesday, 25 April, the police got word that the Marconi station recently erected by the admiralty was to be attacked and some of the principal houses raided. There was consternation at this report, as the wireless operators were unarmed, and there were only seven soldiers to guard the station, while the police force, under Sergeant Burke, to whose energy and ability throughout the week a warm tribute must be paid, was wholly inadequate to protect the town. [38]

When it came to the possibility of an attack on Skerries, the question is how likely was it to occur? Before answering that question, an indication of the wireless station's importance comes from local resident and schoolteacher Paddy Halpin, who, in a memoir, recorded that a message sent from there was 'the first intimation the British government in London had of the Rising' in Dublin.[39] In view of that, the wireless installation was not only of importance in military terms but presumably it would have been a prize for Ashe to have knocked it out of action. Several sources provide evidence that it was in his plans long before the 1916 Rising began. In November 1914, when manoeuvres by Ashe's men and some Dublin City Volunteers occurred at Broadmeadow estuary, near Swords, a mock attack on Skerries was an integral part of the military exercises played out there.[40] In 1915, Dublin Volunteer Liam O'Carroll recalled participating in Volunteer exercises where 'a rather extensive exercise … was held at Skerries, and the Fingal Battalion held it against our attack'.[41] This incident might have been that recorded by the county inspector who put it thus:

> A large contingent of the city Sinn Fein section proceeded to Rush and Lusk railway station where they detrained and were met by contingents from Lusk, Donabate, Swords and Skerries in the county Dublin. 100 had bicycles and 250 were on foot. Those on bicycles went on to Skerries where they stacked their bicycles and scattered on the different roads leading out of Skerries to attack the 250 on foot who were the invading party. Subsequently the various contingents returned home.[42]

In Easter Week 1916, Volunteer Bernard McAllister recorded his having been with a section of the Fifth Battalion heading towards Lusk, when it was suddenly halted at Turvey Hill, about half way on the short journey, after hearing news that British troops had landed at Skerries, and were heading in their direction. After a while spent discussing the matter the section turned around and went in another direction altogether.[43] A press report from the time stated that Lusk 'had the reputation of being a hot-bed of Sinn Féiners', and information was received where 'it was definitely stated that the rebels were on their way to Skerries'.[44] Daire Brunicairdi added that on Tuesday night, 25 April, 'The rear admiral at Larne had signalled to Kingstown that information had been received that the W/T (wireless-telegraph) station at Skerries would be attacked that night'. It appears that at one point in time that it had been 'reported that 800 rebels were only a few miles away, on their way from Donabate to Rush … so great was the alarm that some of the townsfolk left their houses, and paced the shore as the safest place in case of a raid'. [45] Some of the loyalists of the town began to make preparations for any injuries which might come about with the arrival of the rebels. This included 'Captain Battersby, on sick leave, wounded, who took command of the small force in charge of the wireless station. Miss Battersby, with the assistance of Miss McGusty, Misses Clifford and Dr Healy, organized a Red Cross hospital in the Carnegie library'.[46] Further information about Battersby records that on 17 March 1916, he and his wife had attended a recruitment rally at Balbriggan, where certificates of honour were handed out to the relatives of soldiers from that town then serving at the war front. In addition, Battersby was, in April 1914, a member of the South Dublin Unionist Registration Association. Because he made an excuse for the absence of Lord Holmpatrick at a meeting, it can be said that he was a member too.[47]

Brunicardi continued:

> The news from Skerries was causing concern. The Volunteers [led by Thomas Ashe and Dick Mulcahy] were active in the area. … At 2 a.m. on Wednesday [the vessel] *Boadicea* 11 [this number could be either two or eleven] was ordered to proceed there at full speed and render any assistance possible; she could use her gun, but was not to land any men. She arrived at 1 p.m. and signalled that the W/T station was guarded by seven soldiers armed with rifles and ten operators. She also signalled that Portrane and Donabate post offices and Donabate railway station had been destroyed. In the course of the day various alarming messages were to arrive, mainly through the signal station at Larne, concerning the situation at Skerries.[48]

Some of the townspeople sought vantage points to watch:

> A Destroyer was seen steaming at a great pace from Lambay Island. As she drew nearer, it was seen that she was crowded with soldiers. A rush was made by the townsfolk to the harbour, and in a very few minutes

boatloads of military were quickly rowed to the pier, and two hundred men of the North Staffordshire's, under the command of Captain Clay, were landed and marched to the wireless station, where they entrenched in the ditches surrounding the station. The town was saved, and in the offing two gunboats patrolled, their guns being within reach of the coast roads, by which the rebels were expected to arrive. [49]

Brunicardi added that 'on Wednesday evening, when the vessel *Dee* completed guarding the advance on Dublin, she embarked 170 troops and took them to Skerries'.[50] Other sources stated that:

Two gun-boats patrolled [the coastline], their guns being within reach of the coast roads by which the rebels were expected to arrive. On Thursday, 27th April, the Stafford's dug themselves in, put up barricades of carts and sandbags on all the roads leading into Skerries, and made every preparation for a siege. The Harristown and Ashbourne rebels were stated to have joined the Lusk contingent, but if this were so they must have received news of the military force which had landed, and of the guns of the warships trained on the town and roads, and come to the conclusion that discretion was the better part of valour, as the next news was that they had returned to Dublin. The scare was consequently at an end. The North Staffords remained some time in Skerries, and nearly twenty persons were arrested and sent to Dublin.[51]

On Thursday, 27 April, 'as soon as troops became available, a detachment was sent by sea from Kingstown (Dun Laoghaire, Co. Dublin) to Arklow to reinforce the garrison at Kynoch's explosives works, and a small party was sent to assist the RIC post over the wireless station at Skerries'.[52] Because of an unfortunate accident on a military rifle-range there, in which a private Dellowze of the Royal Irish regiment was killed in the days before 8 July 1916, it can be determined that there was a military presence in situ until at least that date or longer.[53]

3. The battle of Ashbourne

The battle at Ashbourne is accepted by some historians as being the most important event outside Dublin city during Easter Week, 1916. Fearghal McGarry wrote that 'Dublin's Fifth Battalion was responsible for the most lethal military engagement outside the capital'.[1] However, F.X. Martin felt that the activities of the battalion commanded by Ashe 'was on a very modest scale consisting of the capture of four small police barracks and the ambushing of a column of police-cars bringing RIC re-enforcements to the barracks at Ashbourne'. He went further by describing Desmond Ryan's account in his *The Easter Rising: the complete story of Easter week 1916*, and of what happened at Ashbourne, as being tantamount to 'sheer exaggeration'. Neither did he share the view that the methods used by Ashe and Mulcahy in Easter Week had great military importance.[2]

On Friday, 28 April 1916, James Connolly, then in the GPO garrison, issued the following statement:

> Soldiers; this is the fifth day of the establishment of the Irish Republic, and the flag of our country still floats from the most important buildings in Dublin, and is gallantly protected by the officers and Irish soldiers in arms throughout the country. Not a day passes without seeing fresh postings of Irish soldiers eager to do battle for the old cause … Our commandants around us are holding their own … the men of north Co. Dublin are in the field, have occupied all the police barracks in the district, destroyed all the telegram system on the Great Northern railway up to Dundalk, and are operating against the trains of the Midland and Great Western. Dundalk has sent 200 men to march upon Dublin, and in other parts of the North our forces are active and strong.[3]

There were plans for the Volunteers in Louth and Meath, led by Donal O'Hannigan, to link up with those in counties Dublin, Kildare and Wicklow, to collectively 'form a ring around the city [Dublin]'. The ring would extend from Swords to Blanchardstown, Lucan and Tallaght, and across the Wicklow hills to the sea. The objective was to prevent or slow-down troops being brought into Dublin from the west.[4] In north Co. Dublin, Joseph Lawless put the strength of the Fifth Battalion at 45 men, all with bicycles. In Easter Week the battalion was engaged in:

a series of lightning raids upon R.I.C. barracks and communications in the area, with the threefold purpose of collecting some much needed arms, hampering enemy movements, and drawing some enemy attention away from the hard-pressed Volunteers fighting in the city.[5]

He named the men sent on the Tuesday from the Finglas camp to support the city garrisons as having been: Capt. Richard Coleman, Daniel Brophy, James Crenigan, William Wilson, Thomas Peppard, William Doyle, Dick Kelly, Peter Wilson, Jack Kelly, John McNally, William Doyle, Edward Lawless, James Wilson, Joe Norton, John Clarke, Patrick Kelly, James Marks and William Meehan.[6] Ann Matthews has added that Arthur Agnew recalled that five Fingal men arrived that evening to assist the rebels then fighting at Kelly's Corner, and they were: Ned Lawless, Daniel Brophy, Jack Kelly, Jack Hynes and Peter Caddell.[7] Another portion of the original group went to the Mendicity Institute, and these were: Richard Coleman, Joe Norton, John Clarke, W. Meehan, T. Peppard, J. Marks, J. Crenigan and the Wilsons and Kellys.[8] Another source for names of those sent to bolster city garrisons was provided by Joseph E.A. Connell jnr.[9]

Skerries men who participated in Dublin garrisons were named by Bairbre Curtis, who gleaned them from the '1916 roll of honour' held in the National Museum, Dublin. These were: Robert Beggs, Joseph McGuinness, Thomas O'Reilly, William Fox, James Shiels, Joseph Derham and William Woodcock. John O'Connor added that some of these served in the Jacob's factory, Four Courts and GPO garrisons.[10] However, Woodcock, according to his daughter-in-law, did not come to live at Skerries until the late 1920s.[11] Derham was a member of 'F' Company, First Battalion, Dublin Brigade, and while in the GPO he was assigned the job of garrison time-keeper by former Fenian, Thomas Clarke. He was given a watch borrowed from a mail bag for that purpose. In later years, having failed to locate the owner he then had it inscribed thus 'Given by order of Tom Clarke to Joseph Derham, during the occupation of G.P.O. 1916' (see front cover).[12]

In Easter Week Ashe and Mulcahy were operating in an information vacuum until the arrival on Wednesday evening at their Kileek camp of Cumann na mBan Volunteer Mary 'Molly' Adrien. She had brought with her Tuesday's issue of the *Irish War News* and a copy of Pearse's 'Proclamation' for their perusal. It was then that the men became aware of how bad the situation was in the city, and also that the country as a whole had not risen. Molly played an important part in the success of the Fifth Battalion, and her obituary of July 1949 records that she had 'a distinguished record with that organization (the Cumann na mBan) … and had carried dispatches from the leaders in the GPO to Thomas Ashe … all that week'. Her name is found on the GPO garrison roll of honour for 1916.[13] Seán Ó Luing saw her as 'a heroine ranking

Leabharlanna Poiblí Chathair Bhaile Átha Cliath
Dublin City Public Libraries

with the bravest'.[14] In several sources she is credited with having brought the news to Thomas Ashe to begin the Rising in north Co. Dublin on Easter Monday, but that is contradicted by Joseph Lawless' account where he stated that it was his aunt Mary, who was also a member of Cumann na mBan and lived in the city, who brought that important news from Pearse.[15]

A few others came to the camp on that Wednesday evening, including Michael Fleming, his sister Dot (who later married Joseph Lawless), Jerry Golden, W. Walsh and P. Holohan.[16] On the next day, Thursday, Michael McAllister said that there was 'some grousing among a section of our men who were complaining that the rest of the country had not risen'. After discussing the matter, Ashe and Mulcahy agreed that those who wished could leave, but they were not to bring anyone else with them. Some did go, but they left their weapons behind them.[17] Gerry Golden outlined the newly reorganized battalion as being made up of Ashe as commandant, Frank Lawless, quartermaster, Captain James V. Lawless, and Captain Richard Hayes as battalion doctor. The rank and file consisted of 35 men from the Swords, Lusk, Skerries and St Margaret's companies. There were Lieutenant Dick Mulcahy, Tom Maxwell, and Paddy Grant, who were from the Second Battalion of the Dublin Brigade. From 'B' Company, First Battalion, Dublin Brigade, were Paddy Holohan, Peadar Blanchfield and his brother Tom, Arthur O'Reilly, and Willie Walsh from Liverpool.[18] On the Friday morning, 28 April, at about 9 a.m., Ashe ordered two sections of men 21 strong, to go with him and Mulcahy and proceed towards the Slane to Ashbourne road. Golden recalled that:

> When about five yards from Rath Cross-roads, we were ordered to dismount and the commandant ordered 11 of the men under orders of Joe Lawless and Charlie Weston, to enter the fields on the north side of the road and proceed under cover of the hedges and ditches until they came to the rear of the Kilmoon RIC barracks … when in position, they were to signal and then Ashe and Mulcahy would go down to the front of the barracks, and call for the police to surrender, otherwise they would be attacked … I was handed two home-made bombs and given instructions in how to use them. I later threw a bomb against the barracks window and lots of glass was smashed … Mulcahy ordered that the second bomb be thrown … The police surrendered, but while waiting for them to come out, the sound of motor cars was heard coming over the brow of a hill further up the Slane Road.[19]

According to Michael McAllister, it was Peter Blanchfield who threw the bombs at the barracks, demonstrating that evidence laid down years after any event occurred cannot completely be relied upon.[20] Terence Dooley pointed to an example where an account by Paddy Holohan 'is littered with inconsistencies and exaggerations'.[21] The original objective on that Friday morning, according to Joseph Lawless, was:

> To travel to Batterstown, 10 miles to the west, to disrupt the Midland and Great Western railway serving Athlone and Dublin, in order to stall troop movements into the city. Three sections, consisting of 39 men, set off from the Borranstown camp but that along the way were side-tracked in raiding the barracks near Ashbourne.[22]

Terence Dooley pointed to 'a mobilization order signed by Thomas Mac Donagh on 3 April 1916 [which], outlined plans for an attack on Ashbourne and other barracks in the surrounding area' to prevent police or military reinforcements from accessing the capital city.[23] The Ashbourne barracks had, 'following four days of intense fighting in the capital', been augmented with extra police from Navan, Dunboyne and Slane, so that by the time of the attack there were nine RIC men and a district inspector stationed there'.[24] It might have been the case, as suggested by Dooley, that 'the barracks had obviously got word to Navan that it was under siege and at 11 a.m. County Inspector Alexander Gray had assembled a force of between 54 and 67 men at Slane to go to the relief of Ashbourne. They packed themselves into 17 motorcars'.[25] The number of cars, and police men, varies, and Joseph Lawless gave it as 24 cars, and 60 to 70 police.[26]

Golden states that the police were equipped with 5-shot magazine carbines of Lee Enfield pattern, bayonets, and revolvers.[27] Joseph Lawless summarized his side's arsenal as follows:

> Modern service rifles including long and short Lee Enfield and 9 millimetre Mauser ... 12 to 15. Old type Mauser (Howth rifle) ... 10 to 12. Martini Enfield single shot carbine ... 12 to 15. Single barrel 12 bore shot guns ... 20 to 30. Revolvers and pistols, various types and calibres (.45, .38, .25) ... 12 to 14. Ammunition: total available in the unit; .303 and 9 millimetre about 100 rounds per weapon. Old Mauser, about 60 rounds per weapon. Shot-gun loaded with buckshot about 300 rounds per weapon. Pistol ammunition, various, about 30 rounds per weapon. Uniform and equipment: about fifteen to twenty men, including most of the officers, had uniforms. The remainder wore their equipment: bandolier, haversack and belt, over their civilian clothes. Bicycles: most of the men of the unit owned bicycles. Transport: one horse and farm dray belonging to my father (Frank Lawless), was the only heavy transport until the commandeering on Wednesday of a Ford motor bread-van. In addition to this there was a Morris Oxford two-seater belonging to Doctor Hayes, and a motor cycle belonging to Thomas Ashe. Explosives: 60 lbs gelignite which was used to destroy the

G.N.R. line on Easter Monday. There remained two home-made canister grenades and some 5 or 6 lbs of gelignite.[28]

Despite the odds being stacked in the RIC's favour, Mulcahy felt that the police 'had walked into a trap and had no chance of success'.[29] That bold assertion might not have been grounded in fact, but perhaps its intention could have been to lift the morale of his men just before the coming fight? As the police reinforcements arrived, Ashe sent men to 'dash towards the Rath Cross and try to stop the RIC from reaching it'. These were Michael Fleming, Dick Aungier, Michael McAllister, Bartle Weston and Bennie McAllister.[30] When in position, Michael McAllister felt that they had excellent sightlines of where the police were sheltering, mainly behind their stalled vehicles. He put the number of cars at about 100, and it was these targets that they fired upon with good results from the start. He wrote that:

> After the initial burst of fire by us, our men settled down very calmly and, although this was our first experience of being under fire, they were behaving as veterans. They were not firing wildly or wasting their ammunition but deliberately picking their targets and dealing with them very coolly in their own time. I was satisfied that whatever would be the outcome of the fight the RIC would have a lot of casualties.[31]

Mulcahy was with the main section located to the rear on the Borranstown road, but came up and asked Charlie Weston 'how many policemen were up the road'. When told about 100, Mulcahy retorted that 'pity it is not a thousand. I will deal with them fellows. Do not let them get down below the cross-roads'.[32] Richard Hayes, while waiting on the police to surrender at the Ashbourne barracks, heard a cordon of cars coming near Rath Cross. The first thought in his mind was that Sean Boylan's group, who were expected to join the battalion during that week, had finally come from Co. Meath. However, Hayes later recorded that 'an immediate volley from the cars quickly disillusioned me'.[33] He knew then that he and the Fifth Battalion had a fight on their hands.

From the start, despite their having had the element of surprise on their side, and being a larger and better armed force, occupying the higher ground, the RIC made themselves easy targets. Furthermore, their constant movements trying to improve their positions did not help their cause. Dooley pointed out that 'as the first RIC man stepped from the leading motor car he was cut down by [Michael] McAllister. Sergeant Shanagher was one of the next to be killed in a hail of bullets. A few of the RIC jumped into the drain cuttings of the bank but these were all killed or wounded in the very early stages of the fight'.[34] This situation continued for hours while the police were pinned down in vulnerable positions all the while. Having lost the leadership of some of their officers who had been killed or wounded, it was inevitable that confusion should reign among the remaining policemen. In their frustration, a number of them discarded their weapons. Michael McAllister put it that 'we now ceased firing … and advanced up the road. The enemy fire had died out completely now and there seemed to be no further fight left in them. The police now came out … with their hands up and we herded them together to a central position where we were joined by Mulcahy and Ashe'.[35] The confusion was not confined solely to the RIC side and there were occasions when the Volunteers, due to being either partially or wholly hidden by bushes, had begun firing upon those on their own side.[36] The closeness of the fighting was such that Joseph Lawless was able to see district inspector Harry Smyth shoot at his father, Frank, only for the bullet to kill John Crinigan instead. Then, in quick reply, Frank Lawless shot Smyth in the head, which led to his instant and gruesome death.[37]

At one point in the afternoon, such was the mayhem that Ashe thought about withdrawing his force but Mulcahy persuaded him to fight on. Joseph Lawless felt that 'Ashe had come to rely on Mulcahy's judgment and capability, accepting his advice without question'. Because of their good relationship Mulcahy could work 'coolly and confidently, without seeming in any way to usurp Ashe's authority as the commander'.[38] Hayes noticed that after the fight had begun, that Mulcahy demonstrated his military knowledge with regard to tactics, and that Ashe appeared happy to engage with him on such matters. Both leaders moved from group to group and gave orders to each in turn.[39] At about 4 p.m., according to Golden, Mulcahy gave orders to charge down the road with bayonets fixed to confront the police as they went along. The tactic was the last straw for the police and some sought shelter in a labourers cottage, where 'we immediately opened fire … as they huddled together … and after about ten minutes, we heard the shout, we surrender … the commandant, [Ashe], then ordered the firing to cease'.[40]

All the wounded received treatment from Dr Hayes, assisted by Molly Adrien and the Murray girls from Garristown, who had only just come on the scene. Before being allowed to leave, Ashe warned them 'of the consequences should any of them be found again in arms against us'.[41] An important recollection by Hayes was that before leaving a policeman had told him that the RIC order for that day was to shoot on sight any rebels encountered and that no prisoners were to be taken.[42]

The official response to the events at Ashbourne came from General J.G. Maxwell, commander-in-chief of the military forces in Ireland, who stated that RIC constabulary inspectors Gray and Smith along with eight constables had lost their lives and 14 were wounded.[43] Those who died were: District Inspector Henry Smyth, Sergeant John Young, Sergeant John Shanagher,

Constables James Hickey, James Gormley, Richard McHale and James Cleary. Along with these, three civilians killed were J.J. Carroll, J. Hogan and a Mr Kepp, the chauffeur of the Marquis Conyngham, Slane Castle. It is likely that the last participant to die was Inspector Gray, who despite suffering terrible injuries as the result of a 'close range shotgun blast' lived until 10 May 1916.[44] On the rebels' side, John Crenigan, Roganstown, Swords, and Thomas Rafferty from Lusk lost their lives. The wounded rebels were: Joseph Taylor, Swords, Jack Rafferty, Lusk, W. Walsh, Dublin, Matt Kelly, Corduff and Edward Rooney from Lusk.[45] When the matter of the Ashbourne incident was raised on 1 June 1916 in the British house of commons, Herbert Samuel announced that the RIC had been overcome by 300 rebels and having exhausted their ammunition they had little choice but to surrender.[46]

After their victory, Ashe brought his men to their Borranstown camp and the sentries were told to be vigilant as it was 'anticipated that there might be an immediate reaction by an enemy force' in the hours ahead. One man on sentry duty was Joseph Lawless and he recalled that a number of men not attached to the battalion arrived. His feeling was that 'most of them were Volunteers who had not answered the call on Easter Monday, but now felt that their place was with us'. These might have been Matt Derham and his cohorts from Skerries. Some others whom Lawless knew had not up till then been Volunteers had also arrived. All the newcomers took up positions as sentries and allowed those already on duty to be relieved. When thinking about the battalions achievements on that Friday at Ashbourne, Lawless recorded his thoughts in the following way:

> Today had been our baptism of fire; five-and-a-half hours of extreme nervous tension during which we had not eaten, and during which there was a fair amount of physical exertion, notwithstanding the static character of the fight … it was not until the following day that we could begin to review what had happened at Ashbourne, and it was only then that the full implications of the fight and our decisive victory began to take shape in our minds. We had come through the test of battle victoriously and against a better armed and well-trained force of twice our number. This was something to be proud of, and something to live up to from henceforth. Our morale rose by leaps and bounds; never again would we be overawed by enemy forces; we had seen their feet of clay, and we had proved to ourselves that we were capable of up-holding the fighting tradition of Fingal in our day. Any latent sense of inferiority was dissipated by this new concept in our power over the enemy, and there is no doubt that had we been called upon for further action, this would have been undertaken with confidence and a highly aggressive spirit that was worth a reinforcement of three times our number.[47]

5 Newbarn camp (*c*.2004) from where Ashe's band of rebels surrendered.

The euphoria among the men under Ashe lapsed into disbelief and apathy on hearing the news of Pearse's surrender to the Dublin Castle authorities, but mixed with the hope that the order did not include them. However, when Mulcahy met Pearse at Arbour Hill prison it was confirmed that all commanders, no matter where they found themselves, had to comply with the terms of the unconditional laying down of arms. Apart from those under Ashe, other rebel units were seen in counties Meath, Louth, Galway, Wexford, Clare and Kerry. At the Arbour Hill meeting, Mulcahy found Pearse lying 'on a bed-board in a cell with a table, a glass of water and some biscuits'.[48] Despite his being told that the order included him and Ashe, Mulcahy nevertheless was adamant that he and the Fifth Battalion Volunteers would not be taken into custody as 'mere rowdies'.[49] The official view from the county inspector was that on Sunday 30 April 'this band of rebels, which then consisted of 32, surrendered … and were taken to Dublin. … The rebels are or will be dealt with under the field general court-martials'.[50] A press report stated that 'it was not until 30th April, that I was to spare a mobile column to deal with this body of rebels, the leaders of which were secured'.[51] The place from where they had been taken into custody was at sheds at Newbarn, near Kilsallaghan. These were still in situ, albeit perhaps having been re-roofed in the interim, prior to 2004 when they were photographed (fig. 5).[52]

On 2 May, Hayes, Ashe and Frank Lawless were held in a large room at Richmond Barracks, Dublin, along with some 20 to 30 other prisoners primarily from the city. Word got about among them that 'all court-martialled prisoners were to say at their trials that going out on Easter Monday they were

6 Memorial at Rath Cross, Ashbourne, Co. Meath
(courtesy of the *Meath Chronicle*).

merely obeying as Volunteers, the orders of their leaders to mobilize in the
ordinary way for manoeuvres'.[53] While Ashe's force was relatively late in being
brought into custody, it was not the last, as that accolade belonged to the Irish
Volunteers at Irishtown, Dublin, where 'a close cordon [was] in place' up to 5
May 1916.[54]

The experiences some of these who left the Newbarn camp before the
cavalry came to take the others into custody are known. Michael MacAllister
wrote that he and his brother and Thomas Weston went on the run in north
Co. Dublin. Michael afterwards made his way to America as a 'coal-trimmer'
on a ship which sailed to New York.[55] Tommy McArdle went on the run in
his own area and Paddy Holohan also got away to America.[56] Thomas Weston
and Bernard McAllister were apprehended and interned in Frongoch.[57]
McArdle, on the other hand, seems to have stayed out of the clutches of the
police and his name was not found on any arrest or release documents. The
two men of that surname on a list compiled by E.A. Connell, Jr, had city
addresses and do not appear to have had any connection with north County
Dublin.[58]

The battle of Ashbourne, and its significance, was not forgotten by the
people of counties Dublin, Meath and perhaps beyond. This was demonstrated,
when, on Easter Sunday, 26 April 1959, the monument at Rath Cross,

Such was the removal of men that the coun
of May 1916 'the whole county [Dublin] is
from the rebellion … the Irish Volunteers are
and they must have been practically wiped o
Volunteers, these still exist as hitherto, but are

Figure 7 shows the places where north (
Only one is given for Dartmoor but there :
source states that about 12 prisoners received
for their participation in the Rising, and wei
but it names only Eoin MacNeill.[9] Sean O N
from Richmond barracks to Kilmainham Ja
1916 … Along with sixty-five others he was t
23 May … he remained there for six months
Lewes Prison'.[10]

All 114 interned men were Roman Cathc
Skerries had the youngest and oldest men, i
William Ganly (aged 64). Swords had the lar
were less than 30 years of age, with 18 men i
16 and Skerries had 12. Of those aged 30 years
had 8, while Swords had 5. Other aspects of
status and occupations, and in the former case
preponderance of single men; for those that v
that 83 were single, while the number of ma
of the 24 men for whom details are available
more mixed profile as between single and r
category, and 3 in the latter. When it came
occupations predominate, and these were 27
farmer's with their sons at 22 and 21 respectiv
where no work details are available, it is prol
have been labourers. Among the 26 occupati
four shop assistants, and none working in fac
of factory workers is curious in that such w
textile industries at Balbriggan. Bairbre
preponderance of labourers among the Volunt
was then a 'largely rural society'.[11] With regar
Gaynor recorded that Balbriggan had little or

By early August 1916, the majority of a
released. In November, the Dublin Castle auth
from the RIC and the Dublin Metropolitar
deciding which of the remaining prisoners s
which should be held for longer. The inform
men, or women, was used to classify each into
are seen in a letter from the Irish under secr
the Irish Office in London. It began:

Ashbourne, Co. Meath, was unveiled by President Séan T. O'Kelly (fig. 6).[59]
An inscription states:

> Erected by the members of the Fingal Brigade old I.R.A., to
> commemorate the victorious battle which took place near Ashbourne
> 28 April 1916 where Volunteers John Crenigan & Thomas Rafferty gave
> their lives. Designed from the poem let me carry your cross for Ireland
> Lord. Composed by their leader commandant Thomas Ashe.[60]

4. After Pearse surrendered

After the Rising of Easter Week, General Sir John Maxwell overs[aw a series] of executions beginning on 3 May, and continuing until 12 [May] by which time 15 leaders of the insurrection had been put to de[ath. These] were: P.H. Pearse, Thomas J. Clarke, Thomas MacDonagh, James [Connolly,] Joseph Plunkett, John McDermott, Edmund Kent, Edward Dal[...] O'Hanrahan, William Pearse, John McBride, Cornelius Colbert[,...] Mallin, J.J. Heuston and Thomas Kent. The first seven had signe[d the] declaration for Irish freedom. John Dillon, MP, when speaking in [the house] of commons on 11 May 1916 warned:

> You are letting loose a river of blood ... It is the first rebellio[n that] took place in Ireland where you had the majority on your si[de ... It is the] fruit of our life work ... and now you are washing out our [...] work in a sea of blood.[1]

Frank Robbins, a Volunteer under James Connolly, concurred wi[th the view] that the British Government had made a 'great mistake ... In ex[ecuting the] leaders'.[2] As Emmet O'Connor put it, 'General Maxwell's exec[utions and] arrests dispelled indignation at the "pro-Germans" and, in an enti[rely different] sense, made Pearse's "blood sacrifice".[3] In human terms, the offici[al ...] arising from the event had, by 20 May 1916, cost the lives of 3[0 ...] police and civilians. Nearly 1,000 others were wounded.[4]

After the general surrender ordered by Pearse, the majority of th[ose ...] were taken into custody under the Defence of the Realm Act, whi[ch allowed] the authorities to arrest people without the need to issue charges aga[inst them.] Details of those arrested, and where in Britain they were sen[t, were] published primarily, but not only, by the *Irish Times* and the *Weekly* [...] In 1917, all the reports were collated and published in the *Sinn Fé[in]* handbook; the majority of all those apprehended from the north C[o. Dublin] area passed through Richmond Barracks, before either being releas[ed or sent] onwards for internment in British prisons. Among the 114 prisoner[s ...] who where deported, there were a number from Skerries who we[re sent to] England from Arbour Hill Prison, rather than having been pr[ocessed at] Richmond Barracks. In general, men from Ireland found themsel[ves in] detention centres at Knutsford, Stafford, Wakefield, Wandsworth, Pert[h,] Woking, Lewes and Dartmoor.[6] While no men from north C[o. Dublin were] executed, some did get death sentences. In all cases these sente[nces were commuted]

to penal servitude, which in some instances, like Thomas Ashe, was [...] [Tab]le 4 gives details of where the interned men from north Co. Dublin [came], along with the number from each of 16 locations.

Table 4. Places from which the 114 interned men came

(26)	Swords	(25)	Skerries	(20)	Castleknock	(7)
(5)	Artane	(5)	Howth	(4)	Finglas	(4)
(3)	Sutton	(3)	Baldoyle	(3)	Cloghran	(3)
(2)	Blanchardstown	(2)	Balbriggan	(1)	Malahide	(1)

[...]amp, North Wales, did not open for Irish political prisoners until [...]6, though it held German prisoners of war before then. Figure 7 [gives de]tails of those sent to prisons other than Frongoch. A press report [...]

constabulary are grabbing at anybody they think they would like [to have] out of the way, whether there is any evidence against the man [or not] ... It must be remembered that the Irish Nationalists have for a [gene]ration regarded the police force as an instrument of oppression, and [the s]udden activity of the force after the years of Mr Birrell's don't lock [them] up policy has roused something of the old bitterness. The [una]uthorized execution of Mr Sheehy-Skeffington has served to [inten]sify this feeling, and the curious situation has arisen that, while the [Sinn] Féin Rising was not a Nationalist rebellion, and was a defiance of [the] Nationalist party, there is now a widespread Nationalist sympathy [with] persons arrested as Sinn Féiners.[7]

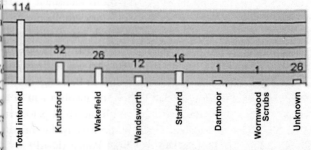

[Places] of detention in Britain for north Co. Dublin men after the 1916 [Ri]sing (but before Frongoch Prison Camp opened on 9 June)

Total interned 114; Knutsford 32; Wakefield 26; Wandsworth 12; Stafford 16; Dartmoor 1; Wormwood Scrubs 1; Unknown 26.

[Pri]sons, Knutsford, Chesshire; Wakefield, West Yorkshire; Wandsworth, South [...] London; Dartmoor, Devon; and Wormwood Scrubs, London.

7 Places where north Co. Dublin men were interned.

Ashbourne, Co. Meath, was unveiled by President Séan T. O'Kelly (fig. 6).[59] An inscription states:

> Erected by the members of the Fingal Brigade old I.R.A., to commemorate the victorious battle which took place near Ashbourne 28 April 1916 where Volunteers John Crenigan & Thomas Rafferty gave their lives. Designed from the poem let me carry your cross for Ireland Lord. Composed by their leader commandant Thomas Ashe.[60]

4. After Pearse surrendered

After the Rising of Easter Week, General Sir John Maxwell oversaw a series of executions beginning on 3 May, and continuing until 12 May 1916, by which time 15 leaders of the insurrection had been put to death. These were: P.H. Pearse, Thomas J. Clarke, Thomas MacDonagh, James Connolly, Joseph Plunkett, John McDermott, Edmund Kent, Edward Daly, Michael O'Hanrahan, William Pearse, John McBride, Cornelius Colbert, Michael Mallin, J.J. Heuston and Thomas Kent. The first seven had signed the 1916 declaration for Irish freedom. John Dillon, MP, when speaking in the house of commons on 11 May 1916 warned:

> You are letting loose a river of blood … It is the first rebellion that ever took place in Ireland where you had the majority on your side. It is the fruit of our life work … and now you are washing out our whole life work in a sea of blood.[1]

Frank Robbins, a Volunteer under James Connolly, concurred with the idea that the British Government had made a 'great mistake … In executing our leaders'.[2] As Emmet O'Connor put it, 'General Maxwell's executions and arrests dispelled indignation at the "pro-Germans" and, in an entirely ironic sense, made Pearse's "blood sacrifice".[3] In human terms, the official estimate arising from the event had, by 20 May 1916, cost the lives of 300 soldiers, police and civilians. Nearly 1,000 others were wounded.[4]

After the general surrender ordered by Pearse, the majority of those arrested were taken into custody under the Defence of the Realm Act, which allowed the authorities to arrest people without the need to issue charges against them.[5] Details of those arrested, and where in Britain they were sent to, were published primarily, but not only, by the *Irish Times* and the *Weekly Irish Times*. In 1917, all the reports were collated and published in the *Sinn Féin rebellion handbook*; the majority of all those apprehended from the north Co. Dublin area passed through Richmond Barracks, before either being released, or sent onwards for internment in British prisons. Among the 114 prisoners (all male) who where deported, there were a number from Skerries who were sent to England from Arbour Hill Prison, rather than having been processed in Richmond Barracks. In general, men from Ireland found themselves sent to detention centres at Knutsford, Stafford, Wakefield, Wandsworth, Perth, Glasgow, Woking, Lewes and Dartmoor.[6] While no men from north Co. Dublin were executed, some did get death sentences. In all cases these sentences were commuted to penal servitude, which in some instances, like Thomas Ashe, was for life. Table 4 gives details of where the interned men from north Co. Dublin came from, along with the number from each of 16 locations.

Table 4. Places from which the 114 interned men came

Lusk	(26)	Swords	(25)	Skerries	(20)	Castleknock	(7)
Donabate	(5)	Artane	(5)	Howth	(4)	Finglas	(4)
St Margaret's	(3)	Sutton	(3)	Baldoyle	(3)	Cloghran	(3)
Ashtown	(2)	Blanchardstown	(2)	Balbriggan	(1)	Malahide	(1)

Frongoch camp, North Wales, did not open for Irish political prisoners until 9 June 1916, though it held German prisoners of war before then. Figure 7 provides details of those sent to prisons other than Frongoch. A press report stated that:

> The constabulary are grabbing at anybody they think they would like to have out of the way, whether there is any evidence against the man or not ... It must be remembered that the Irish Nationalists have for a generation regarded the police force as an instrument of oppression, and the sudden activity of the force after the years of Mr Birrell's don't lock them up policy has roused something of the old bitterness. The unauthorized execution of Mr Sheehy-Skeffington has served to influence this feeling, and the curious situation has arisen that, while the Sinn Féin Rising was not a Nationalist rebellion, and was a defiance of the Nationalist party, there is now a widespread Nationalist sympathy with persons arrested as Sinn Féiners.[7]

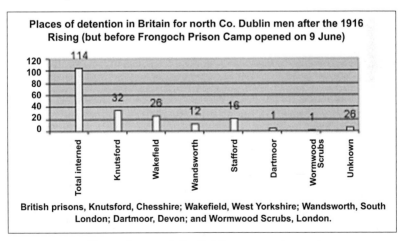

Places of detention in Britain for north Co. Dublin men after the 1916 Rising (but before Frongoch Prison Camp opened on 9 June)

British prisons, Knutsford, Chesshire; Wakefield, West Yorkshire; Wandsworth, South London; Dartmoor, Devon; and Wormwood Scrubs, London.

7 Places where north Co. Dublin men were interned.

Such was the removal of men that the county inspector felt that by the end of May 1916 'the whole county [Dublin] is peaceable and recovering slowly from the rebellion ... the Irish Volunteers are believed to have ceased to exist and they must have been practically wiped out. With regard to the National Volunteers, these still exist as hitherto, but are quite inactive'.[8]

Figure 7 shows the places where north Co. Dublin men were interned. Only one is given for Dartmoor but there may well have been more. One source states that about 12 prisoners received long sentences of imprisonment for their participation in the Rising, and were sent there before 1 June 1916, but it names only Eoin MacNeill.[9] Sean O Mahony recorded that Ashe went from Richmond barracks to Kilmainham Jail for 'court-martial on 11 May 1916 ... Along with sixty-five others he was then transferred to Dartmoor on 23 May ... he remained there for six months after which he was next sent to Lewes Prison'.[10]

All 114 interned men were Roman Catholic. Their age profiles show that Skerries had the youngest and oldest men, from Joseph Shiels (aged 13) to William Ganly (aged 64). Swords had the largest concentration of men who were less than 30 years of age, with 18 men in that category, while Lusk had 16 and Skerries had 12. Of those aged 30 years or over, Lusk had 7 and Skerries had 8, while Swords had 5. Other aspects of the internees are their marital status and occupations, and in the former case, the most striking feature is the preponderance of single men; for those that we have information on we find that 83 were single, while the number of married men was only 9. At Lusk, of the 24 men for whom details are available, all were single. Skerries had a more mixed profile as between single and married, with 17 in the former category, and 3 in the latter. When it came to occupational profiles, three occupations predominate, and these were 27 labourers, with skilled men and farmer's with their sons at 22 and 21 respectively. Of the large number of men where no work details are available, it is probable that many of these would have been labourers. Among the 26 occupations identified, there were only four shop assistants, and none working in factory employment. The absence of factory workers is curious in that such work was readily available in the textile industries at Balbriggan. Bairbre Curtis pointed out that the preponderance of labourers among the Volunteers was to be expected in what was then a 'largely rural society'.[11] With regard to Balbriggan, Volunteer John Gaynor recorded that Balbriggan had little or no involvement in the Rising.[12]

By early August 1916, the majority of all interned prisoners had been released. In November, the Dublin Castle authorities used information collated from the RIC and the Dublin Metropolitan Police (DMP) with a view to deciding which of the remaining prisoners should be given early release, or which should be held for longer. The information about individual interned men, or women, was used to classify each into three categories, details of which are seen in a letter from the Irish under secretary, on 23 November 1916, to the Irish Office in London. It began:

Dear Sir, the chief secretary, before he left for London, directed me to supply him with certain particulars regarding the men residing in areas under my jurisdiction who are now interned in Frongoch. He desired that the men should be placed in three categories, setting forth the degree of danger which would be involved by releasing these individuals from internment ... Class A, consists of men who organized and who would if released continue to organize. In my opinion it is very desirable that these men should not be released at present. Class B, consists of men who deserve punishment, but who are not as important as men in class A. Most of them took an active part in the rebellion, and possibly the question of their release might well be delayed for some little time; each case could thereby be gone into again by the local police; their release depending on the state of the war, and also whether there would still be any possibility of the Germans landing arms or men in this country. Class C, could now perhaps be released provided each person gives the usual undertaking and finds two sureties. Since this return was compiled, a list of all persons interned has been supplied to me by the chief secretary. It includes over 20 names not dealt with in this return, i.e., persons with county addresses who were arrested in Dublin City and who, therefore, were not included by the provincial police in their lists of persons arrested. Inquiry is being made into their history, and, rather than delay the main return, I will in due course submit a supplementary return in regard to these men. I trust this information is what the chief secretary requires.[13]

After finishing their investigations, the overall number of persons was 147 in class 'A'; 80 in class 'B'; and 47 in class 'C'. All the above comes to 274 and out of that figure, some 35 came from north Co. Dublin. This represents fewer than 13 per cent of the whole national figure of 274.

Table 5. Category 'A' prisoners from north Co. Dublin after the Rising: 'Includes leaders, organizers, local leaders, and local organizers, who are prominent extremists and most disloyal'[14]

No.	Name & occupation	Address of prisoner	Police remarks
16	James McDonald, chemist	Skerries	'Active local organizer of Irish Volunteers, who appeared to have plenty of money, but had no employment. Surrendered with the other rebels after Ashbourne to the police'.

No.	Name & occupation	Address of prisoner	Police remarks
14	James Rooney, farmer's son	Lusk	'Active organizer of the Irish Volunteers, whom they collected and led to attack police barracks. Took part in the battle of Ashbourne'.
15	Edward Rooney, farmer's son	Lusk	As above.
17	Joseph Lawless, farmer's son	Swords	'Active local Irish Volunteer organizer. Prominent in attacks on police barracks and was at the battle of Ashbourne'.
18	Edward Lawless, farmer	Swords	'A prominent Irish Volunteer. Went to Dublin with a party of rebels and surrendered there. Two boxes of dynamite found at his house'.
19	John Kelly, labourer	Swords	'An active Irish Volunteer. Took a leading part in the well known Larkin strike some years ago. Went with a party of rebels to Dublin and surrendered there'.
20	Peter Kelly, clerk	Swords	'An active Irish Volunteer. Took part in the attack on police barracks at Swords and Donabate'.
21	Bartle Weston, stonemason	Donabate	'Prominent Irish Volunteer and assisted in organizing. Took part in the attack on police barracks, railway station and post office'.
22	Charles Weston, stonemason	Donabate	'A prominent Irish Volunteer and assisted in organizing. Took part in attack on police barracks, railway station and post office. Also took part in attack on Swords barracks'.
23	Bernard McAllister, farmer	Donabate	'A leader in the attack on Donabate barracks'.

No. of men (10). No. of places represented (4)

The 10 men in table 5 represent nearly 7 per cent of the national figure of 147 in that class.

Table 6. Category 'B' prisoners from north Co. Dublin after the Rising: 'Includes rebels who either took an active part in the rebellion, or who are well known to be extremists of some importance'[15]

No.	Name & occupation	Address of prisoner	Police remarks
28	James Kelly, grocers assistant	Skerries	'Took part in attacks on police barracks and in the Ashbourne battle after which they surrendered when the rebellion collapsed'.
10	John Rafferty, stableman	Lusk	'Took part in the battle of Ashbourne and surrendered to the police subsequently at Newbarn; after the surrender of the leaders in Dublin'.

All below, in two columns, the same as No. 10, above.

No.	Name & occupation	Address of prisoner	No.	Name & occupation	Address of prisoner
11	John McCann, labourer	Lusk	20	James Gough, labourer	Lusk
12	Richard Aungier, carpenter	Lusk	21	Thomas Seaver, van driver	Lusk
13	Richard Kelly, labourer	Lusk	26	Matthew Kelly, farmer	Lusk
14	John Devine, labourer	Lusk	27	Patrick Sherwin, labourer	Lusk
15	James Masterson, labourer	Lusk	25	James Connor, labourer	Swords
16	Joseph Kelly, ward master	Lusk	29	Joseph Taylor butcher	Swords
17	Thomas Kelly, labourer	Lusk	30	Christopher Taylor, drapers assistant	Swords
18	Patrick Doyle, labourer	Lusk	23	Patrick Grant, mechanic	Baldoyle
19	Patrick Brogan, labourer	Lusk			

No. of men (19). No. of places represented (4)

The above 19 men represent nearly 24 per cent of the national figure of 80 in that class. Two men from outside the study area, but who participated with the Fifth Battalion at Ashbourne, are listed in the above class and they were Michael Fleming, Co. Wicklow; and Peter Blanchfield, Carnew Street, Dublin.

Table 7. Category 'C' prisoners from north Co. Dublin after the Rising: 'Includes persons who are not of much importance, who either took part in the rebellion, or had come under notice prior to it'.[16]

No.	Name & occupation	Address of prisoner	Police remarks
43 on DMP list	Joseph Derham, civil-service clerk	Skerries	'Left his lodgings at 26 North Frederick Street (Dublin), on Monday evening and was in the general surrender at the end of that week'.[17]
2	Thomas Taylor, publican	Swords	'Irish Volunteer, but not very dangerous. No evidence of his connection with the actual rebellion'.
3	James Rickard, labourer	Swords	'Irish Volunteer. Did not take part in the actual fighting, but looked after the food supplies'.
4	Thomas Weston, mason	Swords	'Irish Volunteer, but not very Dangerous. Was at Ashbourne'.
5	William Doyle, labourer	Swords	'Not dangerous. Was at the attack on Swords barracks'.
6	Thomas Maxwell, labourer	Baldoyle	'Not dangerous. Was a city Irish Volunteer and surrendered after Ashbourne'.

No. of men (6). No. of places represented (3)

The six men above represent nearly 13 per cent of the national figure of 47 men in that class. Table 8 sums up how many men, in the various categories, came from which places in north Co. Dublin. A single Skerries man, then residing in Dublin, was Joseph Derham, whose details are on the DMP list. All the rest were on the RIC list.

Table 8. Classification of arrested men on RIC and DMP lists, 1916

Places	Class A	Class B	Class C
Baldoyle		1	1
Donabate	3		
Lusk	2	14	
Skerries	1	1	1 (on DMP list)
Swords	4	3	4

There was another list (CM) which dealt with sentenced prisoners who, after courts-martial, were given death sentences, but all later saw their sentences commuted to penal servitude. Those from north Co. Dublin were: Thomas Ashe, Lusk, prisoner number one, a schoolteacher, who got a death sentence that was commuted to penal servitude for life.[18] Richard Coleman, Swords, prisoner number 24, an insurance agent, got a death sentence, commuted to seven years penal servitude.[19] James Crenigan, Swords, prisoner number 33, a labourer, got two years penal servitude, later reduced to one year.[20] James Marks, Swords, prisoner number 108, a labourer, got a death sentence, commuted to three years penal servitude.[21]

After 9 June 1916, many Irish prisoners were removed from a variety of prisons and interned in Frongoch prison camp, situated near the village of Bala in north Wales. After a time, some of them were brought in groups from Frongoch to Wandsworth, or Wormwood Scrubs prisons, London, for interrogation by the Lord Justice Sankey Commission as to their reasons for participating in the rebellion. The interviews, which dealt with individual prisoners in about 15 minutes, proved to have been hardly worthwhile as the prisoners invariably chose not to co-operate. On the other hand, some men were delighted with their having an opportunity to see London, and to see many other places from the train along the way. To some it was akin to an excursion type holiday. At least two north Co. Dublin men went before the commission and these were John 'Rover' McCann and Joseph Lawless.[22]

When Michael Collins wrote to Sean Deasey from Frongoch, he told him that 'I am here and that's the thing that matters. Prating about home, friends and so on doesn't alter the fact that this is Frongoch, an internment camp and that I'm a member of the camp. There's only one thing to do while the situation is as it is, make what I can of it'.[23] Thomas Ashe also appeared sanguine about his being held in Mountjoy Prison, serving penal servitude for life. In a note dated 13 May 1916 to his sister Nora, he wrote:

I am sure you are very much troubled over me for the past few weeks. I expect you know before this of my presence here. The term looks long, but I am facing it in a most optimistic mood. Prison life, so far anyway, is not as bad as one views it from the outside. Be sure and write home as soon as you get this. They must be in a queer state. Let them go on with their business as if nothing happened to me. That is exactly how I look at it.[24]

It appears that such stoicism was not felt by all prisoners in Frongoch. Collins stated that 'the internees faced their imprisonment with an air of dourness, though some … who were innocent of any part in the Rising gave way to despair'. This situation prevailed mainly among 'family men, some of whom suffered from loneliness from their having been abruptly separated from their families'.[25] The experience of Charles Weston is indicative of the travails of more than a few men. He recorded his memories of it as follows:

On Tuesday we were marched to the North Wall and put on a cattle boat down in the hold. … We sailed that night and arrived in Holyhead and from there to Knutsford by train. The boys were in good cheer and sung all the way. I spoke to [Dick], Mulcahy on board the ship and he said that he, was as happy as the day is long, everything is working out grand. On arrival at Knutsford we were put in single cells with bed board and a stool, but no beds. Next evening I got a pillow. After three days I got a very worn blanket. I was about a fort-night there before I got a mattress. We got only half an hour or twenty minutes exercise each day and were not allowed to talk. Food was very bad and the ration was about a quarter enough. After a week we had a bath and a severe haircut. I was never abused however. When about three weeks there we got Mass … and were able to talk a little to one another. … After six weeks in Knutsford we were moved to Frongoch in Wales. Frongoch was good.[26]

When Skerries man, Thomas Hand, wrote an undated letter following his arrest after the 1916 Rising, he had little choice but to write on note-paper provided, which was embossed with the heading 'for God, for King, for Country, Y.M.C.A., H.M. Forces on active service'. The note stated that he was 'prisoner reg. No. 450 C, Thomas Hand, Irish prisoner, Wakefield, c/o chief postal censor, London'. He wrote:

Dear wife … I hope that you and the children are real well and that you are not worrying about me. I am in the best of health and spirits, as are all the boys. Mr Ganly stands the prison well, if old in years he is as young in spirit as any of the men … Your fond husband, Tom.[27]

Another undated letter from Wakefield went:

> Dear wife, hope you are well … I am quite well and in good cheer, and looking forward to the brighter days. All the boys from Skerries are here. You need not send anything to me … I will finish now, asking you to keep up and say a prayer for your ever loving husband, Tom.[28]

By 18 June 1916, Thomas Hand had been transferred to Frongoch prison camp, north Wales, and wrote:

> Dear wife, just a line hoping the children are well and you also as this leaves me … we cannot write more than one letter weekly. I had a parcel from … it came here from Wakefield … tell them not to send stamps or paper as no Irish papers are allowed in here. We are allowed all the letters sent to us … We have a good time here, have control of the camp, our own cooks and postmen, and several committees who manage all the affairs of the camp. We are up at 6 o'clock in the morning and out until 8p.m. in the evening, and then we go to bed at ten o'clock. The weather here is lovely; there are nearly 400 men and more coming … love Tom.[29]

In one more undated letter from Frongoch, Hand wrote 'dear wife … we are permitted to write two letters per week … all the boys from Skerries are here except Joseph Thornton and Joseph Derham … there is a full crowd here now over 1,000 men … Your fond husband Tom'.[30] The letter can be approximately dated because the prison only reached that capacity in July 1916.[31] Hand spoke of having their own postal facility in Frongoch. Thomas Pugh added that he and Joseph Derham (when the latter eventually arrived at Frongoch) were selected to be postmen for the prisoners there.[32] The already mentioned Matt Derham wrote from Frongoch on 26 June, to a Mrs Monks at Skerries, and apologized for his being unable to finish a job of building work, but would do so on his return home.[33] William Ganly, then aged 64 years, was 'the first president of the general council in Frongoch. Sean O Mahony referred to him as 'a veteran nationalist from Skerries … who was appointed at the first meeting of the council on 11 June'.[34] From the council's minute book, it can be seen that Ganly chaired the first meeting on 11 June and it was then that he was elected its president. On 17 June he stated that the function of the council was to look after the 'wants and comforts of the Irish prisoners of war at Frongoch'. Ganly chaired meetings through June and into early July. By then a military council had been formed and it usurped the powers of the general council, which then went into a decline. The last meeting was held on 10 July with Ganly in the chair.[35] Ganly led an interesting life. He was born in Co. Westmeath in *c.*1852, but at some point thereafter he went to Argentina,

South America, where he remained for much of his life. However, by 1901, he and his Co. Westmeath-born wife and Argentine-born adopted son, Peter Gibbons, were resident at Adelaide Road, Glasthule, Dublin. Then, prior to 1907, they were living in Co. Longford, where Ganly got a mention in William Bulfin's work *Rambles in Eirinn*. The relevant passage recorded that Bulfin went 'on to Granard next day, more hills, more woods, and more pleasure. I met William Ganly of Irish Ireland fame and passed a night under his hospitable roof at Creevy House'. Bulfin was editor and proprietor of the *Southern Cross* newspaper, Buenos Aires, Argentina.[36] While living in Longford Ganly led a busy political life until, according to Marie Coleman, 'divisions began to emerge within the United Irish League at the height of the ranch war in mid-1907, with the defection of William Ganly, a leading figure in the league in north Longford, to the nascent Sinn Féin organization'. He did share in some of the successes of the Sinn Féin movement in that county.[37] Perhaps because of the political strife he endured there, by 1911, he had left Co. Longford to live at 3 St Columba's Road, Drumcondra.[38] By *c*.1914 he was living and farming at Baldungan, Skerries. His obituary stated:

> The death of Mr William Ganly on November 17th 1931, removes a prominent Skerries resident from our midst. He was chairman of the Balrothery Board of Guardians, and was one of our local representatives on the Rural District Council up to its dissolution … he was active in public affairs … as chairman of the local Improvements Committee. Most of his life was spent in the Argentine, South America … he took a keen interest in politics and local government affairs, and was a vehement defender of his convictions.[39]

The experiences of Dr Hayes and Joseph Kelly who both worked at the Balrothery Union are interesting. The Union's minutes of 6 May 1916 stated that the men had 'gone missing from their jobs'.[40] A press report on 27 May stated:

> The Local Government Board wrote, noting an entry contained in the minutes to the effect that Dr Richard Hayes, medical officer of the Lusk dispensary district, had absented himself from duty without leave during the previous fortnight and had been suspended from office by the guardians. It appears from the official statement published and verified by the military authorities that Dr Hayes has been convicted by court-martial, due to his having taken part in the recent rebellion, and has been sentenced to 20 years penal servitude; and the L.G.B. [local government board], so as to terminate his connection with the M.O. [medical officer] of the Lusk dispensary district, have issued instructions removing him

from office. As regards ward master, Joseph Kelly, who has also been reported for absenting himself from duty, the L.G.B. informed the guardians that he is at present detained in Knutsford detention barracks, and on receiving further particulars they will again address the guardians on the subject. A sealed order from the L.G.B. signed by Sir H.A. Robinson, announced Dr Hayes dismissal.[41]

It appears that there was scant sympathy for the doctor's predicament, whatever about the other man. When one guardian asked what would happen if Dr Hayes appeared, another replied that 'Hayes has ceased to exist as far as our union is concerned'. Dr Healy of Skerries was asked to act as substitute doctor in his colleague's absence and it was intimated that a permanent position might open up later when the position of Hayes became known.[42] At first glance it could be thought that the board's treatment of the two men was somewhat harsh, but their attitude was a reflection of the common mood after the collapse of the Rising. Perhaps something of this attitude prevailed at Skerries, at least in some quarters. The desire to punish those involved in the Rising is also apparent in an allegation raised in the British house of commons, on 29 June 1916, by Mr Alfred Byrne MP, who asked whether:

> The under-secretary of the state for war if he can state what part Lord Holmpatrick took in the Curragh revolt two years ago; if he can say whether Lord Holmpatrick took an active part in inciting the military against the Government at that time; if he is aware that Lord Holmpatrick is evicting some of his tenants; and if he is aware that the reason given is because their sons took part in the rising and that the Government desire them to be punished.
>
> [Mr Tennant replied] I know nothing about the matters referred to in the first two parts of the question, but it is, I think, common ground that it is undesirable to rake over the events at the Curragh of two years ago. The relationship between Lord Holmpatrick and his tenants is, obviously, not a matter with which the War Office has anything to do.[43]

In relation to the alleged attempt at evicting tenants, as no further information could be found, there the matter must rest. However, it seems that it was a regular occurrence in the town that whenever the tension was raised above a certain level, the Holmpatrick monument (fig. 2) was targeted and damaged, usually having tar daubed over it. This happened in October 1914 and a court case was still going on in March 1916, at the quarter sessions court at Balbriggan.[44] The monument was again tarred on the night of 14 June 1915, and the railings were also interfered with. Three men were charged on this occasion: James Landy, Edward Brady and Joseph Beggs. The first mentioned was acquitted and the other two got off under the first offenders act, but with a reprimand. It was said that the gravity of the offence was 'accentuated by the fact that it was committed when Lord Holmpatrick is wounded at the war front'.[45] The aforementioned Beggs was one of those arrested at Skerries after the collapse of the Rising and was sent to Wakefield on 6 May, and afterwards transferred to Frongoch, where he remained until his release on 21 July 1916.[46] He got a mention in the press for having played a football game there on 16 July. He and a number of Co. Dublin prisoners, one of whom was Dan Brophy from Lusk, played against a team of Wexford prisoners in a mock championship; the Dublin side won the match.[47] While the game itself could be seen as a frivolous affair, it does show that the inter-county rivalry which applied in such games at home also pertained in Frongoch.

If Holmpatrick had considered evictions for tenants with sons interned, then one of them might have been the Beggs family who lived at Hoar Rock, Skerries. In relation to Holmpatrick's army career, details in a letter written by a Private Smith, who was stationed at the Curragh in May 1914, is informative. According to Smith, H.W. Holmpatrick (1886–1941) had been a lieutenant, then a captain, before becoming a special reserve officer acting as adjutant of the 16th Lancers. He resigned his commission on 19 May, but returned to the job in August 1914. In March of that year, as a colonel, he was one of those who refused to act against the Unionists in Ulster, the so-called 'Curragh incident'.[48]

Skerries was again in the news in the aftermath of the Rising, when, on Monday, 9 July 1917, the widow of Thomas MacDonagh, whose husband had been executed in the previous year as a leader in the rebellion, drowned while on holiday in that town. Muriel MacDonagh was a 31-year-old mother of two young children who, as a consequence, were orphaned. She was a sister of Grace Gifford, widow of Joseph Plunkett, also executed after the Rising. On the day after Muriel's death, a special Mass was celebrated at Skerries, where among those who came from the city, where she had lived, were Rory O'Connor, Fred Allen and the Revd Albert, ASFC, who officiated at the ceremony. Afterwards, her coffin, draped in the Sinn Féin colours, was carried to the train station by Irish Volunteers from Skerries, Lusk and Rush. It was stated to have been one of the largest funeral processions ever seen in the town with an estimated 1,000 people having followed it to the station, from where her body was removed to the Pro-Cathedral in Dublin. On the following Thursday her remains were taken by way of her south Dublin home before proceeding to Glasnevin cemetery for burial. Prior to her unfortunate accident, Muriel had intended to stay at Skerries for the month of July, along with other widows of executed men, namely, James Connolly, Joseph Plunkett and Eamon Kent.[49]

The dust had hardly settled before another tragedy occurred, this time with the death of Thomas Ashe, from the effects of his being force-fed in Mountjoy prison. He became seriously ill, was moved to the Mater hospital, and died there on 25 September 1917. Soon after his death, the British guards melted away, and the Irish Volunteers took control and these included those from Fingal who took their turn to 'guard their dead leader'. Ashe's body was afterwards removed to the Pro-Cathedral for solemn requiem Mass, before it lay at Dublin's City Hall until Sunday 30 September when it was interred at Glasnevin cemetery.[50] Though his demise was a loss to the Irish Volunteer movement, then undergoing a re-organization, it nevertheless presented the movement with an opportunity of raising its profile, as had previously been done with O'Donovan Rossa's funeral in 1915. The military arrangements for Ashe's removal were undertaken by his erstwhile colleague, Richard Mulcahy, and many thousands lined the streets of Dublin and onwards to the burial ground at Glasnevin.[51] Tricolours flew everywhere along the procession route and, according to Éilis Ní Chorra, there was no police presence observed on the streets along the way.[52] In the procession, which took a route from City Hall, through Dame Street, Thomas Street, Bridgefoot Street, North Quays, Batchelor's Walk, O'Connell Street and onwards to Glasnevin, the Lusk Black Raven Pipers band was to the fore, and sympathizers from Drogheda, Balbriggan, Skerries, Lusk and other centres were present, having arrived by train. A contingent from Kerry had pride of place and entered the cemetery immediately following the chief mourners. Catholic priests, Hoey, PP, and Toher, CC, Lusk, were also there. However, it appears that only one member of the Irish Parliamentary Party made an appearance, and that was Alderman Alfred Byrne, MP.[53] For those who could not be there on the day, Masses were

8 Volleys over Thomas Ashe's grave (courtesy of Fingal Co. Library on Local Studies Archive).

celebrated at Skerries, Donabate and Drogheda.[54] After Ashe's body was laid in the ground, volleys of rifle shots were fired over the grave (fig. 8). Michael Collins in the oration said that 'nothing additional remains to be said. That volley which we have just heard is the only speech which is proper to make above the grave of a dead Fenian'.[55] The involvement of the Dublin Brigade 'raised the movements profile and led to its renaissance'.[56] A little over a year later, in December 1918, Richard Coleman passed away from an illness while in Usk prison. This saw the Dublin Brigade once again in the limelight.[57] Peter Hart pointed out that despite the 'Rising's crushing defeat ... the movement got stronger and gained further credibility and paramilitarism got a second chance because the government provided it'.[58]

As has been mentioned above, around the time of Ashe's demise, there was a renewed interest in reforming Irish Volunteer and Sinn Féin companies. In north Co. Dublin this also occurred and at Skerries, a meeting of a Sinn Féin Company was held on 18 November 1917, with William Ganly in the chair. Speakers such as J. Stanly, Patrick, Mathews and Frank, Lawless gave their views, while Count Plunkett told the gathering that 'the Irish people should rely on themselves, and not on parliamentary action'. Furthermore, they should pledge themselves 'to secure an Irish Republic. No self-respecting Irish man could be satisfied with anything less'.[59] Among the officers of the above company were Irish Volunteers already mentioned in this story – John 'Terry' Sherlock, Jack McGowan and Matt Derham. There were newcomers, one of whom was James Murray, a man who described himself 'as the man in the gap' between that which had already gone and that which had yet to come. He and others participated in the re-established Skerries Volunteer Company in early 1918. Examples of those willing to come on board the new company were Charles and Joseph Kelly and Charles Murray.[60] Thomas Peppard and John Gaynor pointed out that fledgling companies were forming or contemplating forming at Swords, Donabate, Lusk, Balbriggan, St Margaret's, Finglas, Oldtown and Garristown.[61]

Conclusion

There is little doubt but that the Irish Volunteers of north Co. Dublin played an important part in the Easter Rising of 1916, and that those from Skerries were involved in every facet of it. The Skerries men's experiences were intertwined with those of their comrades in arms from elsewhere within the designated area and to tell their story in that way was an important objective by the author from the start. It could be said that had it not been for Eoin MacNeill's countermanding order, their collective impact might well have been greater still. However, interpretations of their significance and that of the Rising as a whole, have varied and one of those who downplayed the events as carried out by Thomas Ashe, Richard Mulcahy, Frank Lawless and Joseph Lawless (who later became a colonel in the Irish army), among others, was F.X. Martin. He claimed that the activity in north Co. Dublin was 'subsidiary to events in the city'. However, it could be suggested and has been by some historians, that the fighting in the city, being more static in nature, was a far cry from the strategy undertaken by Ashe whereby the best utilization of a small force numbering at best 50 men formed into mobile sections, which could move around an area at relative speed, was innovative. The tactics used might have been a precursor to the so-called 'flying columns' used to good effect by the IRA in the War of Independence.

In December 1962, General Richard Mulcahy in *An tÓglach* observed that:

> Fingal was well represented at the (Rotunda Hall) Rink in Parnell Square, on 25 November 1913. They were at Howth; they were also in strength with Pearse and Clark, at the Limerick parade on Whit Sunday, 23 July 1915. At least five Fingal officers were at the Ticknock training camp that summer.[1]

When it comes to an event which has remained fresh in the people's collective memory that which took place on Friday, 28 April 1916, stands out. It was then that Ashe's small force engaged with a larger, better trained and equipped force of RIC at Rath Cross, Ashbourne, Co. Meath, in a fight which has since entered into Irish local and national history as the 'battle of Ashbourne'. This was demonstrated when, in April 1959, a large limestone monument was unveiled by President Sean T. O'Kelly at the site of the battle (fig. 6). He said:

That moment would help to remind the present generation and the generations to come of the efforts and achievements of the men who helped greatly to make Easter Week an effective assertion in arms of Ireland's indefeasible right to national freedom and sovereignty … the aim of Pearse was to end foreign rule in all Ireland: not in twenty or twenty-six counties, but in the whole thirty-two counties which comprised this island. That was still the objective of the vast majority of the people.[2]

Taking into account two broader viewpoints, the first being from Róisín Higgins, who put it that 'for many in Ireland, 1916 has become shorthand for the Easter Rising. This underlines the extent to which that event displaced all others of that year, most notably and contentiously the battle of the Somme'.[3] The second view comes from Augustine Birrell, the former Irish chief secretary, who made his feelings on the matter plain when he wrote in 1936 that 'as a rebellion it was a ridiculous failure from the first, but as an event in Irish history it was horrible and heartbreaking and … a supreme act of criminal folly on the part of those who were responsible for it … it was really nothing more than a Dublin row'.[4]

From this short narrative, it has been seen that the Volunteers of Skerries had played a constructive part in the events as they unfolded. At least two, and more likely three of them, Peter Gibbons, James McDonnell and Joseph Kelly fought with Ashe's Fifth Battalion in Easter Week, including in the battle of Ashbourne, while some others such as Matt Derham participated after the fighting was already over. One man, Jack McGowan suffered the indignity of having been sent home because he was too young to fight. Other Skerries Volunteers fought with city battalions under the auspices of the Dublin Brigade, and took orders from Pearse, Connolly, and other leaders whose lives were soon to be extinguished by executions in the days and weeks after the rebellion was crushed. The Skerries men, 20 strong, were among the 114 men identified here as having been arrested and sent for internment in Britain. While in prisons such as Wakefield, Stafford and Frongoch, to name just three, they wrote letters home which now provide insights as to how they dealt with prison life, what conditions were like, and how they maintained morale. Their stoic attitude seems to have been, on the whole, more concerned with their loved ones at home than on their own predicaments. Some, like William Ganly made themselves useful while in Frongoch. Sean Ó Mahony thought highly enough of Ganly to describe him as 'a veteran nationalist from Skerries … who was appointed at the first meeting of the council on 11 June' 1916.[5] However, it might have been stretching it a bit to call him a Skerries man, because he was first and foremost a Westmeath man, he was born there, and after he died his remains returned for burial there as he had wished.

The so-called Howth Mauser rifle played an important part in the years before and during the Rising. Of the Skerries haul of 50 rifles obtained at Howth, only a few can be located now. Some may still be in the possession of the families of Volunteers. Two came to light in *c.*1970 when the old home of Matt and Joseph Derham, at Hoar Rock, Skerries, was being demolished and the Howth rifles were found hidden in the thatch. One is now in the possession of Cork Museum, The Mardyke, Cork, having been deposited there in 1971.[6] Michael McAllister commented on the rifles describing them as 'cumbersome articles … they had no magazine, being single shot weapons. Yet in our innocence we were very proud of them'.[7]

Leabharlanna Poiblí Chathair Bhaile Átha Cliath
Dublin City Public Libraries

Appendix[1]

The names of the 114 arrested men from north Co. Dublin after the 1916 Rising. The places shown are in order of size and numbered from one to 16. Other details associated with the men, such as age profiles, marital status, etc. are found in my MA thesis.

(1) Lusk (26 men)
Ashe, Thomas
Brogan, Patrick
Brophy, Daniel
Carroll, Patrick
Caddell, Patrick
Devine, John
Gough, James
Hayes, Richard F.
Hynes, John
Kelly, Dick
Kelly, Matthew
Kelly, Thomas
Kelly, Joseph

Masterson, James
Meehan, William
Menally, John
Murphy, Francis
McCann, Jack
McNally, John
Rafferty, John
Rooney, James
Rooney, Edward
Rungien, Richard
Peppard, Thomas
Seaver, Thomas
Sherwin, Patrick

(2) Swords (25 men)
Crenigan, James
Coleman, Richard
Doyle, William
Duff, Thomas
Early, Patrick J.
Kelly, Joseph
Kelly, Peter
Lawless, Frank J.
Lawless, Edward
Lawless, Joseph
Marks, James
Manning, P.

Moran, Peter
Moran, Christopher
Norton, Joseph
Nugent, Christopher
Rickard, James
Ryan, T.
Stafford, Edward
Taylor, Joseph
Taylor, Thomas
Taylor, Christopher
Weston, Thomas
Wilson, James
Wilson, William

(3) Skerries (20 men)
Beggs, Joseph
Derham, Robert
Derham, Matthias
Derham, Joseph
Duffe, Anthony
Ganly, William
Gibbons, Peter
Hand, Thomas
Keane, Peter
Kelly, Joseph

Lacey, Michael
Maguire, Dennis
McDonnell, James
McGuinness, Joseph
O'Reilly, Thomas
Reynolds, J.H.
Shanley, Michael
Sherlock, John
Shiels, Joseph
Thornton, Joseph

(4) Castleknock (7 men)
Bennet, T.
Dowling, A.
Dowling, J.
Duffy, Christopher
English, Patrick
Mooney, John
Mooney, Patrick

(5) Artane (5 men)
Christie, Peter
Joyce, John
Lamgare, Patrick, (Lanigan)
Murphy, John
McDermott, Owen

(6) Donabate (5 men)
Collins, Edward
McAllister, Bernard
McAllister, Daniel J.
Weston, Bartle
Weston, Charles

(7) Finglas (4 men)
McKee, Richard
Moloney, J.
O'Higgins, Brian
Tanning, M.

(8) Howth (4 men)
Bowen, Barth
Reddin, Gerard
Reddin, Kenneth
Reddin, Thomas

(9) Baldoyle (3 men)
Grant, Patrick
Gough, J.
McDonough, J.

(10) Cloghran (3 men)
Lawless, James V.
O'Connor, James
Ryan, P.

(11) St Margaret's (3 men)
Duke, Thomas
Duke, Richard
Riley, Thomas

(12) Sutton (3 men)
Maxwell, Thomas
Mulcahy, Richard
Nolan, M.

(13) Ashtown (2 men)
O'Driscoll, Robert
Robinson, Thomas

(14), Blanchardstown (2 men)
McNulty, M.
McNulty, Patrick

(15) Malahide (1 man)
O'Connell, James

(16) Balbriggan (1 man)
Madigan, James

Notes

ABBREVIATIONS

BMH,WS   Bureau of Military History,Witness Statements, 1913–1921. Military
                      Archives, Dublin
CM   Commuted (penal sentence)
CSORP   Chief Secretary's Office Registered Papers (NAI)
DMP   Dublin Metropolitan Police
IMA   Irish Military Archive
IRA   Irish Republican Army
IRB   Irish Republican Brotherhood
NAI   National Archives of Ireland
NLI   National Library of Ireland
RIC   Royal Irish Constabulary
SHS   Skerries Historical Society
TNA   The National Archives, Public Record Office, London
UCDA   University College Dublin, Archives Department
UVF   Ulster Volunteer Force

INTRODUCTION

1   Séamas Ó Maitiú, *Dublin's suburban towns,
1834–1930: governing Clontarf, Drumcondra,
Dalkey, Killiney, Kilmainham, Pembroke,
Kingstown, Blackrock, Rathmines and
Rathgar* (Dublin, 2003), pp 140–1.

2   Patrick Archer, Bob Brown and Jarlath
Duffy (eds), *Fair Fingall* (Fingal, 1975),
p. 1.

3   Maighréad Ni Mhurchadha, *Fingal,
1603–60: contending neighbours in north
Dublin* (Dublin, 2005), p. 24.

4   Samuel Lewis, *A topographical dictionary
of Ireland, comprising the several counties,
cities, boroughs, corporate, market, and post
towns, parishes, and villages*, 2, vols,
(London, 1837), i, pp 78, 100–1, 211; ii,
pp 420–21, 583–4. Ask about Ireland,
http://www.askaboutireland.ie
(accessed, 18 Mar. 2013).

5   Joseph Byrne, *War and peace: the survival
of the Talbots of Malahide* (Dublin, 1997),
p. 8.

6   *Thom's Almanac and general directory,*
(Dublin, 1916), pp 1893, 1735, 1771,
1890, 1898.W.E.Vaughan and A.J.

Fitzpatrick (eds), *Irish historical statistics:
population, 1821–1971* (Dublin, 1978), p. 29.

7   Joseph Byrne (ed.), *Fingal Studies*, 1
(Summer, 2010), pp 1–33, 34–49, 50–70.

8   Fearghal McGarry 'Keeping an eye on
the usual suspects: Dublin Castle's
personality files, 1899–1921', *History
Ireland*, 14:6 (Nov–Dec. 2006), 44.
Military Archives, Dublin; IMA, BMH
WS. Available online at
http://www.militaryarchives.ie/collecti
ons/online-collections/bureau-of-
military-history-1913-1921

9   Raymond Gillespie, 'An historian and
the locality' in Raymond Gillespie and
Myrtle Hill (eds), *Doing Irish local
history: pursuit and practice* (Belfast, 1999),
pp 12–14.

10   Bulmer Hobson, *Defensive warfare: a
handbook for Irish Nationalists* (Belfast,
1909), pp 26, 28–9; cited in Oliver
Snoddy, 'National Aid 1916–1917–
1918', *Capuchin Annual*, 33 (1966), 331.

11   For further details see P.F. Whearity,
'The Irish Volunteers in north Co.
Dublin, 1913–17', (MA thesis, National
University of Ireland, Maynooth, 2011).

1. A BRIEF PREAMBLE TO THE 1916 RISING

1 *An Claidheamh Soluis*, 1 Nov. 1913.
2 R.V. Comerford, *Ireland* (London, 2003), p. 174.
3 *Volunteer Gazette*, Dec. 1913: cited in Bulmer Hobson, *A short history of the Irish Volunteers, 1913–1916* (Dublin, 1918), p. 39. *Freeman's Journal*, 21 Nov. 1913. F.X. Martin (ed.), *The Irish Volunteers, 1913–1915, recollections and documents* (Dublin, 1963), pp vii–xi, 98–108.
4 *Freeman's Journal*, 26 Nov. 1913. Hobson, *A short history of the Irish Volunteers*, pp 20, 26–8.
5 Richard Mulcahy (UCDA, Mul. P, p7/D/29); cited in Maryann Gialanella Valiulis, *Portrait of a revolutionary: General Richard Mulcahy and the founding of the Irish Free State* (Dublin, 1992), pp xi, 3, 5–6, 7. Ronan Fanning, 'Mulcahy, Richard' in *Dictionary of Irish biography* (Cambridge, 2009). http://dib.cambridge.org. (accessed, 11 Oct. 2011).
6 Hobson, *A short history of the Irish Volunteers*, pp iii, 15.
7 Seán Ó Luing, *I die in a good cause; a study of Thomas Ashe, idealist and revolutionary* (Tralee, 1970), pp 10, 21–25. C.J. Woods and William Murphy, 'Ashe, Thomas (Tomas Aghas)', *Dictionary of Irish biography* (Cambridge, 2009), http://dib.cambridge.org. (accessed, 10 Oct. 2011).
8 Sean O Mahony, *The first hunger striker, Thomas Ashe, 1917* (Dublin, 2001), pp 5–6.
9 Jack Baker, 'The townland of Balcunnin', *Time & Tide* 6 (2008), 91–2.
10 Frank Whearity, 'Thomas Hand, 1878–1920, Irish Volunteer' in *Time & Tide* 4 (2001), 46–7, 66. Sean O Mahony, *Frongoch: university of revolution* (Dublin, 1987), p. 223.
11 County Inspector's Confidential Monthly Report, TNA, CO904/93, part 4, May 1914.
12 *Irish Times*, 8 Apr. 1914.
13 *Drogheda Independent*, 31 Jan., 7 Feb. 1914. *Freeman's Journal*, 6 Feb. 1914.
14 Skerries Historical Society 'overview of Skerries history, part 2."

15 www.oldskerries.ie (accessed, 1 Apr. 2013).
15 D.P. Moran (ed.), *The Leader*, Sept. 1911; cited in Paddy Halpin, 'D.P. Moran's views on Skerries', SHS paper No. 108, read in 1975.
16 *Irish Independent*, 2 Dec. 1913. (It is not clear from the source whether these were two separate companies or one combined unit.)
17 *Meath Chronicle*, 21 Mar. 1914. Inspector General's Confidential Monthly Report, TNA, CO904/93, part 4, May 1914. *Dundalk Democrat*, 28 Feb., 9 May 1914. Donal Hall, *World War I: and nationalists politics in County Louth, 1914–1920* (Dublin, 2005), pp 13–15.
18 *Freeman's Journal*, 10 Dec. 1913, 24 Apr. 1914. Census of Ireland, 1901–1911. *Irish Times*, 30 Aug. 1915.
19 *Drogheda Independent*, 31 Jan., 7 Feb., 9 May 1914. *Freeman's Journal*, 6 Feb., 25 May 1914. *Irish Independent*, 25 May 1914. *Irish Times*, 25 May 1914. Census of Ireland, 1901–1911. County Inspector's Confidential Monthly Report, TNA, CO904/93, part 4, May 1914.
20 Inspector General's Confidential Monthly Report, TNA, CO904/93, part 4, May 1914.
21 Terence Dooley, *Inniskeen, 1912–1918: the political conversion of Bernard O'Rourke* (Dublin, 2004), p. 27.
22 Peter Cahalan, *Belgian refugee relief in England during the Great War* (London, 1982), p. 27. E. Moberly Bell, *Flora Shaw* (London, 1947), pp 278–9; cited in Peter F. Whearity, 'Belgian refugees in Ireland during World War One', *Ríocht na Midhe*, 20 (2009), 253.
23 David Fitzpatrick, *Politics and Irish life, 1913–1921: provincial experiences of war and revolution* (Dublin, 1998), p. 88.
24 *Freeman's Journal*, 11 June 1914.
25 *Irish Times*, 8 Apr. 1914. County Inspector's Confidential Monthly Report, TNA, CO904/93, part 4, Apr.–May 1914. *Irish Independent*, 25 May, 3, 10 June 1914. *Freeman's Journal*, 13 June 1914. *Drogheda Independent*, 9, 23 May 1914.
26 *Irish Times*, 27 July 1914. *Irish Independent*, 27 July 1914. *Freeman's Journal*, 27 July

1914. Bernard McAllister, Bureau Military History, Witness Statement, (IMA, BMH, WS 147).

27 Frank Whearity, 'Thomas Hand, 1878–1920, Irish Volunteer', *Time & Tide*, 4 (2004), 48–9.

28 *The Times*, 27 July 1914.

29 County Inspector's Confidential Monthly Report, TNA, CO 904/94, part 4, July 1914.

30 Hobson, *A short history of the Irish Volunteers*, p. 9; cited in Diarmaid Ferriter, *The transformation of Ireland, 1900–2000* (London, 2004), p. 127.

31 *Royal commission into the circumstances connected with the landing of arms at Howth on July 26th, 1914. Minutes of evidence with appendices and index*, ii, 8, 830 [Cd. 7649], HC 1914–16, xxiv, 830, 863. Originals in www.british parliamentarypapers.com (accessed, 10 Oct. 2011); copies held at Fingal Co. Co. Library and Local Studies Archive, Swords, Co. Dublin.

32 Paddy Halpin, 'Memories of the monument', SHS paper No. 138, read in 1984.

33 *Drogheda Independent*, 1, 8, Aug. 1914; *Freeman's Journal*, 22 July 1914.

34 *Irish Times*, 8 Apr., 6 July 1914. *Irish Independent*, 25 May, 3, 10 June, 6, 14 July, 5 Aug. 1914. *Drogheda Independent*, 9, 23 May, 27 June, 11, 25 July, 1, 8, 15 Aug. 1914. County Inspector's Confidential Monthly Report, TNA, CO904/93, part 4, Apr.–May 1914. *Freeman's Journal*, 13 June, 10 July 1914. County Inspector's Confidential Monthly Report, TNA, CO904/94, part 4, July 1914.

35 *Drogheda Independent*, 3, 24 Oct. 1914. County Inspector's Confidential Monthly Report, TNA, CO904/94, part 4, Aug. 1914. McAllister, '1916 contemporary account of some events in Fingal', p. 56. Risteard Ó Colmáin, 'Memories of 1916' in Bernadette Marks (ed.), *Swords Voices*, 1: 6 (1998), p. 31. County Inspector's Confidential Monthly Report, TNA, CO904/94, part 4, Sept. 1914. Christopher Moran, IMA, BMH, WS 1438. Charles Weston, BMH, WS 149. *Freeman's Journal*, 3 Oct. 1914. Autographed letter by J.V. Lawless

(about the Santry Company 1914. NLI, MS 41,652/1). County Inspector's Confidential Monthly Report, TNA, CO904/95, part 4, Oct. 1914.

36 *Drogheda Independent*, 1, 8, 15 Aug. 1914.

37 Weston, IMA, BMH, WS 149; cited in Christopher Fox, 'Recollections of 1916 in Skerries', paper No. 143, read in 1985; cited in Bairbre Curtis, 'Fingal and the Easter Rising 1916', *Fingal Studies*, 1, (2010), 38.

38 McAllister in, '1916 contemporary account of some events in Fingal' in Rena Condrot, Pat Hurley and Tom Moore (eds), *Old tales of Fingal* (Fingal, 1984), p. 56.

39 *Freeman's Journal*, 10 Oct. 1914; cited in Bernard Howard, 'The British army and Fingal during the Great War', *Fingal Studies*, 1 (2010), 3.

40 *Drogheda Independent*, 24 Oct. 1914.

41 F.X. Martin, 'Writings of Eoin MacNeill', *Irish Historical Studies*, 6 (Mar. 1948), 227–8.

42 *Irish Independent*, 14–15 Jan. 1953.

43 *An tÓglach*, 1: 6 (Dec. 1962), 1.

44 *Dublin Brigade Review* (National Association of the Old IRA, Dublin, 1939), p. 13.

45 Hayes, IMA, BMH, WS 97.

46 Moran, IMA, BMH, WS 1438.

47 *Dublin Brigade Review*, p. 13. *Irish Times*, 2 Aug. 1915.

48 Michael Wheatley, 'Irreconcilable enemies' or flesh and blood? The Irish Party and the Easter rebels 1914–16' in Gabriel Doherty and Dermot Keogh (eds), *1916, the long revolution* (Cork, 2007), p. 61.

2. THE 1916 RISING IN NORTH CO. DUBLIN

1 Brendan Mac Giolla Choille (ed.), *Intelligence notes, 1913–16, preserved in the State Paper Office* (Dublin, 1966), p. 205.

2 County Inspector's Confidential Monthly Report, TNA, CO904/99, part 4, Mar. 1916.

3 Joseph Lawless, 'Fight at Ashbourne', *Capuchin Annual*, 33 (1966), 307. Joseph Lawless, IMA, BMH, WS 1043.

4 Richard Hayes, IMA, BMH, WS 97. Thomas Peppard, IMA, BMH, WS 1399.

5   The 1916 Rising: personalities and
    perspectives, an online exhibition, 7.12.
    Ashbourne, Co. Meath. http://
    www.nli.ie/1916/ (Accessed, 6 Feb.
    2011); cited in Lawless, 'Fight at
    Ashbourne', p. 307; cited in Terence
    Dooley, 'Alexander "Baby" Gray (1858–
    1916) and the battle at Ashbourne, 28
    April 1916', *Ríocht na Midhe*, 14 (2003),
    208.

6   Lawrence W. White, 'Plunkett, Joseph
    Mary' in *Dictionary of Irish biography*
    (Cambridge, 2009), http://dib.
    cambridge.org. (Accessed, 15 June
    2011); Conor Kostick and Lorcan
    Collins, *The Easter Rising: a guide to
    Dublin in 1916* (Dublin, 2000), p. 137.

7   Ann Matthews, *The Kimmage garrison,
    1916: making billy-can bombs at Larkfield*
    (Dublin, 2010), p. 7.

8   Nancy Wyse-Power, IMA, BMH, WS
    541; cited in Frank Whearity, 'The life
    and times of Mary "Molly" Adrien,
    1873–1949, Cumann na mBan
    Volunteer 1916', SHS paper No. 260,
    read in 2006. *Sinn Féin rebellion
    handbook* (Dublin, 1917), p. 7. (Hereafter
    cited as *Reb. handbook*).

9   Hayes, IMA, BMH, WS 97.

10 *Sunday Independent*, 23 Apr. 1916. *Reb.
    handbook*, p. 7. Lawless, IMA, BMH, WS
    1043.

11 Weston, IMA, BMH, WS 149; cited in
    Charles Townshend, *Easter 1916; the Irish
    Rebellion* (London, 2006), pp 139, 215.
    Fearghal McGarry, *Rebels: voices from the
    Easter Rising* (Dublin, 2011), p. 269.

12 Fearghal McGarry, *The Rising, Ireland:
    Easter 1916* (Oxford, 2010), pp 234–5.
    Michael T. Foy and Brian Barton, *The
    Easter Rising* (2nd ed. Stroud, 2011),
    p. 274. Paul Maguire, 'The Fingal
    Battalion: a blueprint for the future' in
    the Military Heritage of Ireland Trust
    Ltd www.militaryheritage.ie/
    (Accessed, Nov. 2012). See also, *Irish
    Sword*, 28:112 (2011), 208–28.

13 Lawless, IMA, BMH, WS 1043; cited in
    Ó Luing, *I die in a good cause: a study of
    Thomas Ashe*, pp 76–7.

14 Lawless, IMA, BMH, WS 1043. Hayes,
    IMA, BMH, WS 97.

15 Weston, IMA, BMH, WS 149. Lawless,
    IMA, BMH, WS 1043. McAllister in,

'1916 contemporary account of some
events in Fingal', p. 57. Townshend,
Easter 1916; the Irish Rebellion, p. 216.

16 Ernie O'Malley, *The singing flame*
    (reprint. Dublin, 1979), p. 131.

17 Frank Robbins, 'Remember Easter
    Week 1916', *Dublin Historical Record*,
    23:2–3 (Dec. 1969), p. 98.

18 *Weekly Irish Times*, 29 Apr. 1916. *Irish
    War News, the Irish Republican* (25 Apr.
    1916).

19 *Reb. handbook*, p. 49.

20 Courtesy of Lillie Derham, Church
    Street, Skerries; cited in Frank
    Whearity, 'Brothers in arms, Matthias
    and Joseph Derham, Irish Volunteers
    1916', *Time & tide* 7 (2010), 128–9.

21 Lawless, IMA, BMH, WS 1043. Lawless,
    'Fight at Ashbourne', p. 308. Hayes,
    IMA, BMH, WS, No. 97.

22 *Midland Tribune, Tipperary Sentinel and
    Offaly County Vindicator, '1916 Rising
    Souvenir Jubilee 1966 Supplement'*, 9 Apr.
    1966; cited in Paul O'Brien, *Field of fire;
    the battle of Ashbourne, 1916* (Dublin,
    2012), p. 20. Census of Ireland, 1901–
    1911.

23 Anne Clare, *Unlikely rebels; the Gifford
    girls and the fight for Irish Freedom* (Cork,
    2011), p. 201.

24 *Sinn Féin rebellion handbook*, p. 77.
    O Mahony, *Frongoch, university of
    revolution*, p. 180.

25 Ó Luing, *I die in a great cause: a study of
    Thomas Ashe*, p. 80.

26 Peadar Bates, *Rebellion in Fingal: the
    preparation, outbreak and aftermath*
    (Donabate, 1998), p. 101.

27 O Mahony, *The first hunger striker:
    Thomas Ashe, 1917*, pp 6–7.

28 Lawless, 'The battle of Ashbourne' in
    *Dublin's fighting story; told by the men who
    made it, 1913–1921* (Tralee, 1949), pp
    60–1.

29 Ó Luing, *I die in a good cause: a study of
    Thomas Ashe*, p. 80. Townshend, *Easter
    1916, the Irish Rebellion*, p. 216.

30 Valiulis, *Portrait of a revolutionary: General
    Richard Mulcahy*, pp xi, 2–3, 5.

31 Lawless, 'The battle of Ashbourne', pp
    60–1. Lawless, 'Fight at Ashbourne', pp
    307–15. Lawless, IMA, BMH, WS 1043.
    O Mahony, *The first hunger striker,
    Thomas Ashe, 1917*, pp 9–10. Noel Tier,

'The 5th Battalion, Irish Volunteers, in Ashbourne, Co. Meath and surrounding areas, Monday 24 to Sunday 30 April 1916', *Ríocht na Midhe*, 21 (2010), 182–3.

32 Lawless, 'The battle of Ashbourne', p. 61.

33 County Inspector's Confidential Monthly Report, TNA, CO, 904/99, part 4, Apr. 1916. Mac Giolla Choille (ed.), *Intelligence notes, 1913–16, preserved in the State paper office*, p. 233.

34 Lawless, 'Fight at Ashbourne', p. 308. Lawless, IMA, BMH, WS 1043. Charles Townshend, *Easter 1916, the Irish Rebellion*, p. 216. *Reb. handbook*, p. 32.

35 *Reb. handbook*, pp 7–10, 31, 34.

36 *Reb. handbook*, p. 11.

37 County Inspector's Confidential Monthly Report, TNA, CO904/99, part 4, Apr. 1916. Mac Giolla Choille (ed.), *Intelligence notes, 1913–16, preserved in the State paper office*, p. 233.

38 *Weekly Irish Times*, 29 Apr. 1916. *Irish Times*, 10 May 1916. *Reb. handbook*, p. 40.

39 Paddy Halpin, 'Some early memories' SHS paper No. 165, read in 1992, p. 18; cited in Clare, *Unlikely rebels: the Gifford girls and the fight for Irish Freedom*, p. 200.

40 Weston, IMA, BMH, WS 149.

41 Liam O'Carroll, IMA, BMH, WS 314.

42 County Inspector's Confidential Monthly Report, TNA, CO904/96, part 4, Jan. 1915.

43 McAllister, IMA, BMH, WS 147.

44 *Weekly Irish Times*, 29 Apr. 1916. *Irish Times*, 10 May 1916. *Reb. handbook*, p. 40.

45 Daire Brunicardi, *The seahound: the story of an Irish ship* (Cork, 2001), pp 41–2.

46 *Weekly Irish Times*, 29 Apr. 1916. *Irish Times*, 10 May 1916. *Reb. handbook*, p. 40.

47 *Irish Times*, 30 Apr. 1914; 20 Mar. 1916.

48 Brunicardi, *The seahound: the story of an Irish ship*, pp 41–2.

49 *Weekly Irish Times*, 29 Apr. 1916. *Irish Times*, 10 May 1916. *Reb. handbook*, p. 40.

50 Brunicardi, *The seahound: the story of an Irish ship*, pp 41–2.

51 *Weekly Irish Times*, 29 Apr. 1916. *Irish Times*, 10 May 1916. *Reb. handbook*, p. 40.

52 *Reb. handbook*, p. 95.

53 *Irish Times*, 8 July 1916.

3 THE BATTLE OF ASHBOURNE

1 McGarry, *The Rising, Ireland: Easter 1916*, p. 234.

2 F.X. Martin, '1916: myth, fact, and mystery', *Studia Hibernica*, 7 (1967), 91–2.

3 *Reb. handbook*, 49–50.

4 Donal O'Hannigan, IMA, BMH, WS 161; cited in McGarry, *The Rising, Ireland: Easter 1916*, p. 211.

5 Joseph Lawless, 'The battle of Ashbourne' in *Dublin's fighting story: as told by the men who made it, 1913–1921* (Tralee, 1949), p. 60.

6 Lawless, IMA, BMH, WS 1043.

7 Arthur P. Agnew, IMA, BMH, WS 152; cited in Matthews, *The Kimmage garrison, 1916: making billy-can bombs at Larkfield*, p. 36.

8 Richard Balfe, IMA, BMH, WS, No. 251. Ray Bateson, *They died by Pearse's side* (Blanchardstown, Co. Dublin, 2010), pp 112–13.

9 Joseph E.A. Connell, *Dublin in Rebellion: a directory, 1913–1923* (Dublin, 2009), pp 390–1.

10 National Museum garrison rolls; cited in Curtis, 'Fingal and the Easter Rising 1916', 41. John O'Connor, *The 1916 Proclamation* (Dublin, 1999), pp 71, 80.

11 Told to author by Mrs Mary Woodcock (daughter-in-law), Dublin Road, Skerries, in Sept. 2012.

12 Recollections of Tom Derham (son), the Kybe, Skerries; cited in Whearity, 'Brothers in arms, Matthias and Joseph Derham', 134.

13 Lawless, IMA, BMH, WS 1043. *Irish Press*, 20 July 1949; cited in Whearity 'The life and times of Mary "Molly" Adrien'. O'Connor, *The 1916 Proclamation*, p. 60.

14 Crenigan, BMH, WS 1395. Weston, IMA, BMH, WS 149; cited in Ó Luing, *I die in a good cause, a study of Thomas Ashe*, p. 81. *Fingal Independent*, 26 Aug. 2005.

15 Lawless, IMA, BMH, WS 1043.

16 Lawless, IMA, BMH, WS 1043.

17 McAllister in, '1916 contemporary account of some events in Fingal', p. 60; cited in McGarry, *The Rising, Ireland: Easter Week 1916*, p. 235.

18 Gerry Golden, IMA, BMH, WS 177.
19 Golden, IMA, BMH, WS 177.
20 McAllister, '1916 contemporary account of some events in Fingal', pp 60–1.
21 Dooley, 'Alexander "Baby" Gray', 227–8, 213. See NLI, Devoy papers, MS 18,098.
22 Lawless 'Fight at Ashbourne', *Capuchin Annual*, 33, 310–11; cited in Dooley 'Alexander "Baby" Gray', 210.
23 Thomas MacDonagh (mobilization order signed Apr. 1916. Allen Library, O'Connell Schools, Dublin); cited in Dooley, 'Alexander "Baby" Gray", 209.
24 John Austin, 'The battle of Ashbourne, 28 April, 1916: an eye-witness statement' in *Ashbourne memorial book* (Dublin, 1959), p. 39; Report on the state of the counties, 1916 (TNA, CO904/120); cited in Dooley, 'Alexander "Baby" Gray" 210.
25 Dooley, 'Alexander 'Baby' Gray', 211.
26 Lawless, 'Fight at Ashbourne', 311.
27 Golden, IMA, BMH, WS 177.
28 Lawless, 'Fight at Ashbourne', 308–9.
29 Lawless, IMA, BMH, WS 1043.
30 Golden, IMA, BMH, WS 177. Lawless, 'Fight at Ashbourne', 308–9. Lawless, IMA, BMH, WS 1043.
31 McAllister, '1916 contemporary account of some events in Fingal', pp 61–2.
32 Ibid., p. 62.
33 Hayes, IMA, BMH, WS 97.
34 Dooley, 'Alexander "Baby" Gray', 213.
35 Lawless, 'Fight at Ashbourne', 313. McAllister, '1916 contemporary account of some events in Fingal', pp 62–3.
36 Dooley, 'Alexander "Baby" Gray', 215.
37 Lawless, IMA, BMH, WS 1043; cited in McGarry, 'Violence and the Easter Rising' in David Fitzpatrick (ed.), *Terror in Ireland, 1916–1923* (Dublin, 2012), pp 46–7.
38 Lawless, IMA, BMH, WS 1043.
39 Hayes, IMA, BMH, WS 97.
40 Golden, IMA, BMH, WS 177; cited in Dooley, 'Alexander "Baby" Gray', 216.
41 Lawless 'Fight at Ashbourne', p. 316. Lawless, IMA, BMH, WS 1043. Weston, IMA, BMH, WS 149.
42 Hayes, IMA, BMH, WS 97.
43 *Irish Times*, 22 July 1916.
44 *Irish Times*, 4 May 1916. Dooley, 'Alexander "Baby" Gray', 217–18. Tier, 'The 5th Battalion, Irish Volunteers, in

Ashbourne, Co. Meath and surrounding areas, Monday 24 April to Sunday 30 April 1916' , 186–7.
45 Lawless, 'Fight at Ashbourne', 316; Desmond Ryan, *The Rising; the complete story of Easter Week* (Dublin, 1949), p. 225. Lawless, IMA, BMS, WS 1043.
46 *Irish Times*, 2 June 1916.
47 Lawless, IMA, BMH, WS 1043.
48 *Irish Times*, 22 July 1916. Joost Augusteijn, *Patrick Pearse: the making of a revolutionary* (Basingstoke, 2010), p. 319.
49 Valiulis, *Portrait of a revolutionary: General Richard Mulcahy*, p. 16.
50 County Inspector's Confidential Monthly Report, TNA, CO904/99, part 4, Apr. 1916.
51 *Irish Times*, 22 July 1916.
52 Hayes, IMA, BMH, WS 97.
53 Richard Hayes, IMA, BMH, WS 876.
54 *Weekly Irish Times*, 27 May 1916. *Reb. handbook*, p. 45. Ronan Fanning, 'Richard Mulcahy', *Dictionary of Irish Biography*, online source.
55 McAllister, '1916 contemporary account of some events in Fingal', pp 65–6.
56 Dooley, 'Alexander "Baby" Gray', 218.
57 O Mahony, *Frongoch, university of revolution*, pp 185, 195.
58 Connell, *Dublin in rebellion: a directory 1913–1923*, p. 391. Ó Mahony, *Frongoch: university of revolution*, p. 185.
59 *Drogheda Independent*, 2 May 1959. Ashbourne memorial book, p. 47. *Irish Times*, 27 Apr. 1959.
60 Bateson, *They died by Pearse's side*, p. 164.

4. AFTER PEARSE SURRENDERED

1 *Reb. handbook*, pp 62, 64. Brian Barton, *From behind closed doors: secret court martial records of the 1916 Easter Rising* (reprint. Belfast, 2003), pp 258–9. Townshend, *Easter 1916: the Irish Rebellion*, p. 269.
2 Robbins, 'Remember Easter Week 1916', p. 100.
3 Emmet O'Connor, *A labour history of Ireland, 1824–1960* (Dublin, 1992), p. 92.
4 *Weekly Irish Times*, 20 May 1916.
5 *Weekly Irish Times*, 29 Apr. 1916.
6 *Irish Times*, 11–16, 18, 25–26 May, 5, 16 June 1916. *Weekly Irish Times*, 20, 27

May, 10, 24 June 1916. *Reb. handbook*, pp 69–86.

7 *Daily Mail*, 14 May 1916. *Sunday Independent*, 14 May 1916.

8 County Inspector's Confidential Monthly Report, TNA, CO 904/100, part 4, May 1916.

9 *Irish Times*, 1 June 1916.

10 Ó Mahony, *The first hunger striker, Thomas Ashe*, pp 16–17.

11 Curtis, 'Fingal and the Easter Rising 1916', p. 44.

12 John Gaynor, IMA, BMH, WS 1447.

13 RIC list of interned rebels, 1916 (NAI, Chief Secretaries Office Registered Papers (Hereafter cited as CSORP, 16627/18).

14 (NAI, CSORP 16627/18).

15 (NAI, CSORP 16627/18).

16 (NAI, CSORP 16627/18).

17 (DMP, list, NAI, CSORP 16627/18); cited in Whearity, 'Brothers in arms, Matthias and Joseph Derham', 134–5.

18 Thomas Ashe, No. 1, on CM. list of 1916 internees (NAI, CSORP 19265/16).

19 Richard Coleman, No. 24 on CM list (NAI, CSORP 19265/16).

20 James Crenigan, No. 33 on CM list (NAI, CSORP 19265/16).

21 James Marks, No. 108 on CM list (NAI, CSORP 19265/16).

22 Lawless, IMA, BMH, WS 1043. O Mahony, *Frongoch, university of revolution* (Dublin, 1987), pp 48, 145–56.

23 Letter from Michael Collins to Sean Deasey, undated; cited in Rex Taylor, *Michael Collins: the big fellow* (reprint. London, 1965), p. 55; cited in Tim Pat Coogan, *Michael Collins: a biography* (London, 1990), p. 50.

24 Ó Luing, *I die in a good cause: a study of Thomas Ashe,* p. 94.

25 Taylor, *Michael Collins: the big fellow,* p. 54.

26 Weston, IMA, BMH, WS 149.

27 Prison letters from Thomas Hand to his wife Rose, Kilmainham Jail Archive; cited in Whearity, 'Thomas Hand, 1878–1920, Irish Volunteer' in *Time & Tide* 4 (2004), 55–8.

28 Ibid.

29 Ibid.

30 Ibid.

31 Barton, *From behind a closed door; secret court martial records of the 1916 Easter Rising*, p. 61.

32 Thomas Pugh, IMA, BMH, WS 397.

33 Whearity, 'Brothers in arms, Matthias and Joseph Derham', 131–2.

34 O Mahony, *Frongoch, university of revolution,* p. 47. Census of Ireland, 1901–1911.

35 Frongoch minute book, original held at O'Connell Schools Archive, Dublin (Accessed on microfilm at the NLI, P.1638); cited in O Mahony, *Frongoch, university of revolution,* pp 47–8, 52.

36 Census of Ireland, 1901–1911. William Bulfin, *Rambles in Eirinn* (reprint, Dublin, 1996), p. 423. Martin, *The Howth, gun-running, and the Kilcoole gun-running, 1914,* p. 150.

37 Marie Coleman, *County Longford, and the Irish revolution, 1910–1923* (Dublin, 2003), pp 18–21, 24, 68, 71, 74.

38 Census of Ireland, 1901–1911.

39 *Drogheda Independent,* 28 Nov. 1931.

40 Balrothery Boards of Guardians minute book (NAI, BG 40, A.139, Apr.–Sept. 1916), p. 85.

41 *Drogheda Independent,* 27 May 1916.

42 Ibid.

43 *Hansard, House of Commons, Parliamentary Debates* (written answer to do with the military service of Lord Holmpatrick, HC Deb, 29 June 1916, Vol. 83). http://hansard,millbank systems.com/ (accessed, 15 June 2011).

44 *Sunday Independent,* 5 Mar. 1916.

45 *Irish Independent,* 30 June 1916.

46 *Irish Times,* 16 May 1916. *Rebellion handbook,* p. 79.

47 *Anglo-Celt,* 29 July 1916.

48 Ian F.W. Beckett (ed.), *The army and the Curragh incident, 1914* (2 vols, Army Records Society, London, 1986), ii, 112, 361, 404. Census of Ireland, 1901–1911.

49 *Irish Times,* 10 July 1917. *Irish Times,* 13 July 1917. *Weekly Irish Times,* 14 July 1917. *Nenagh Guardian,* 14 July 1917. Mary Josephine MacDonagh (NLI, MS 33,567(10), 'news clippings etc., in envelope inscribed Sr Francesca, 1917', regarding the drowning of Mrs MacDonagh at Skerries). Laurence Nugent, IMA, BMH, WS 907. Elizabeth Balcombe, 'Day of the drowning', *Skerries News,* 18:3 (Apr. 2007), 24.

50 Ó Luing, *I die in a good cause* pp 182, 185–6.
51 Death of Thomas Ashe (Cathal Brugha Barracks, Military Archive, A/list, index files. A/0232/1, group vi. Fingal Brigade casualties, 1917–1921). O Mahony, *The first hunger striker, Thomas Ashe*, pp 22–3, 25. Michael Hopkinson, *The Irish War of Independence* (Dublin, 2004), p. 97.
52 Éilis Ní Chorra, 'A rebel remembers', *Capuchin Annual*, 33, 298.
53 *Irish Independent*, 1 Oct. 1917.
54 *Irish Independent*, 9 Oct. 1917.
55 O Mahony, *The first hunger striker: Thomas Ashe*, p. 25.
56 Ashe (Military Archives, A/list, index files. A/0232/1). O Mahony, *The first hunger striker, Thomas Ashe*, pp 22–3, 25. Hopkinson, *The Irish War of Independence*, pp 97–8.
57 *Dublin Brigade Review*, p. 17.
58 Peter Hart, 'Paramilitary politics and the Irish revolution' in Fearghal McGarry (ed.), *Republicanism in modern Ireland* (Dublin, 2003), p. 34.
59 *Irish Times*, 19 Nov. 1917.
60 James Murray, South Strand, Skerries (personal papers held by his son Joe, same address). *Fingal Independent*, 26 Mar. 2004. Census of Ireland, 1901–1911. *Irish Press*, 13 Oct. 1942. Frank Whearity, 'John "Terry" Sherlock Irish Volunteer, 1897–1920', SHS paper No. 228, read in 2002. Whearity, 'Charles and Joseph Kelly, Irish Volunteers in the War of Independence and Civil War' paper read in two parts, the first part in Sept. 2012, and the second part in Nov. 2012. See Skerries Historical Society, http://www.oldskerries.ie/rept1211.html (Accessed on 24 Mar. 2013).
61 Peppard, IMA, BMH, WS 1399. Gaynor, IMA, BMH, WS 1447.

CONCLUSION

1 Richard Mulcahy, 'The work of Thomas Ashe' in Piaras Beaslaí (ed.), *An tÓglach*, 1: 6 (Dec. 1962), pp 1–2, 12.
2 *Drogheda Independent*, 2 May 1959.
3 Roisín Higgins, *Transforming 1916: meaning, memory and the fiftieth anniversary of the Easter Rising* (Cork, 2012), p. 4.
4 Augustine Birrell, *Things past redress* (London, 1937), p. 219; cited in Martin, '1916: myth, fact and mystery', p. 7.
5 O Mahony, *Frongoch; university of revolution*, p. 47.
6 Letter dated 6 Feb. 2004, from Stella Cherry, curator of Cork Public Museum, The Mardyke, to Joseph Derham, Frankfield, Grange, Cork. Whearity, 'Brothers in arms: Matthias and Joseph Derham, Irish Volunteers 1916', pp 143–4.
7 McAllister, '1916 contemporary account of some events in Fingal', p. 56.

APPENDIX

1 *Irish Times*, 11–16, 20, 25, 30 May, 5, 9, June 1916. *Weekly Irish Times*, 20, 27 May 1916. *Sunday Independent*, 14 May 1916. *Irish Independent*, 19 May 1916. *Nenagh Guardian*, 13 May 1916. *Sinn Féin rebellion handbook*, pp 64–91. CM, list of Irish prisoners, 1916 (NAI, CSORP, No. 19265/16). Art O'Briain papers (NLI, MS 8442–8445). Details of Irish prisoners, 1916 (NAI, CSORP, 15564/16). Joseph Murray, a copy of a list of prisoners in north camp, Frongoch, 1916 (NLI, MS 1650). O Mahony, *Frongoch; university of revolution*, pp 176, 181, 183.